PHAIDON GUIDE TO
SILVER

PHAIDON GUIDE TO
SILVER

MARGARET HOLLAND

PHAIDON · OXFORD

Page 1 L to R: Horn, given as an archery prize, John Denzilow, 1791 : Late 19th-century snuff box, incorporating a shell; Gavel, Sheffield, 1870; Figural cream jug, Dutch, 1903.

Page 2: Octagonal tea kettle on a stand with a lamp, by Joseph Ward, London, 1719.

Managing Editor: Giles Lewis
Editor: Howard Loxton
Picture editor: Ann Davies
Designer: Richard Brookes
Production: Elizabeth Digby Firth
Special photography: A. C. Cooper
and Paul Forrester
Line drawings: Stephen Cocking

Paperback ISBN 0 7148 1847 X
Hardback ISBN 0 7148 1846 1

Published by Phaidon Press Ltd,
Littlegate House, St. Ebbe's Street, Oxford

Planned and produced by
Elsevier International Projects Ltd, Oxford.

Filmset by Keyspools Ltd, Golborne,
Lancashire, Great Britain.
Colour origination by Art Color Offset, Rome, Italy
and Colour Workshop, Hertford, Great Britain.
Black and white origination by Jolly and Barber Ltd,
Rugby, Great Britain.
Printed and bound by Brepols, Turnhout, Belgium.

CONTENTS

ACKNOWLEDGMENTS

Unless otherwise stated, all the illustrations on a given page are credited to the same source.

Photographs were supplied by the American Museum in Britain, Bath page 104*tl*; James Charles, London page 154*b*; Christie Manson & Woods page 19, Cooper-Bridgeman Library, London page 90–91, 119, 180*r*, 213*t*, 225; Cooper-Bridgeman Library/Henry Ford Dupont Winterthur Museum page 113*b*, Cooper-Bridgeman Library/Metropolitan Museum of Art, New York page 218*l*, Cooper-Bridgeman Library/ Victoria and Albert Museum page 28, 35, 193*t*; Stuart Devlin page 47; Garrard's page 134, 142; Brand Inglis page 108*l*, 215*b*, M. McAleer page 228*t*; Mansell Collection page 45; Metropolitan Museum of Art, New York; Samuel D. Lee Fund 1938 page 107; Octopus Books page 62*tl*, 101*r*; Sotheby Parke Bernet & Co page 23, 27, 31, 43, 59, 61, 63, 67*l*, 73*b*, 76*b*, 77, 78, 79, 80*t*, 81, 82*b*, 84, 85*b*, 89, 103*c*, 108*r*, 109, 113*t*, 115, 116, 118, 123*t*, 124, 126*b*, 129, 135*t*, 138, 147, 151*l*, 152, 155*t*, 156*r*, 161*b*, 166, 167, 169, 175*l*, 177, 182–3, 185, 191*b*, 192, 193*b*, 208*t*, 212, 217, 221*b*, 227*b*, 232, 233, 239*b*; Spink & Son page 39, 105; Victoria and Albert Museum, Crown Copyright page 17*t*, 22, 25, 29, 64*l*, 65, 67*c*, 71, 75, 83, 95*t*, 117*b*, 163, 184, 219, 220; Louis Wine, Dublin page 111*b*; Worshipful Company of Goldsmiths page 2, 36, 54, 55, 66, 146. Silver was made available for photography by Anne Bloom Antiques page 222*b*, 223; The Button Queen page 203; Brand Inglis page 82*t*, 153, 160, 200, 215*t*; M. McAleer page 1, 110, 119*t*, 137, 164*t*, 173*b*, 194, 195, 196, 199*b*, 201, 206, 208*b*, 209*b*, 211*t*, 213*b*, 215*t*, 228*b*, 235, 236–7, 237*b*, 240; Private collections page 1, 95*b*, 172, 176, 196, 199*b*; S. J. Phillips page 24, 26, 41, 44, 46, 53, 62*bl*, 69, 70, 73*t*, 74, 76*t*, 80*b*, 85*tl*, 85*tr*, 87, 93*t*, 97, 98, 99, 100, 102, 103*t*, 106, 112, 114, 117*t*, 119*c*, 120, 121, 122, 123*b*, 125*b*, 126*t*, 127, 128, 130, 135*b*, 138–9, 141, 144, 145, 150, 159, 161*t*, 162, 164*b*, 165, 181, 182, 183*t*, 186, 187, 189, 190, 191*t*, 199*t*, 202, 205, 207, 210*r*, 211*b*, 222*t*, 224, 229, 230*l*, 231, 236, 237*t*; S. J. Shrubsole page 140, 151*t*, 154*t*, 175*r*, 180*l*, 183*b*, 197, 198, 209*t*, 214–15, 230*r*, 239*t*, 241; Sotheby Parke Bernet & Co page 62–3, 96, 125*t*, 155*b*, 157*b*, Spink & Son page 93*b*, 136, 156*b*, 158, 168, 174–5, 221*t*; C. J. Vander page 1, 110, 210*l*, 238.

PREFACE

This compact guide has been planned to give an understanding of the essential qualities of silver and to enable the reader to recognise the style and period or those pieces that are likely to be seen in the average saleroom, shop or museum.

No short book on silver can do more than show the important developments in Europe and America and the events from which they stem. The migrations of goldsmiths and the spread of techniques and design give the subject world scope, but this book deals largely with the western world, showing the silver of its countries in context with each other so that the reader may find out what a particular object was like at any given time in his own or other countries.

The very old is sketched in lightly to show its important influences, but since silver was so often melted down to be used as currency or remodelled to suit a newer fashion, little of it survives and the majority is to be found in museums today. Examples of such magnificent work are illustrated in the opening chapters while the text, concentrating on general trends, avoids descriptions of specific pieces or the work of a particular goldsmith, aiming to give a more general survey of the subject, and the guide section aids identification of those pieces which are more easily obtainable.

Throughout the book the word "goldsmith" is used to describe the craftsman in gold or silver, a generic term accepted in most countries, describing men controlled by a single governing body, such as the Worshipful Company of Goldsmiths, set up in London in the year 1300, to control all business concerning workmanship in gold or silver.

The Publishers have attempted to observe the legal requirements with respect to the rights of the suppliers of photographic materials. Nevertheless persons who have claims are invited to apply to the Publishers.

INTRODUCTION

The craft of the goldsmith is very ancient. Long ago it spread through the continent of Europe, mainly from the Mediterranean, and far beyond, particularly to Ireland where Celtic tradition in the arts was strong. Unweaving the tangled pattern of the evolution and spread of styles is a task for the archaeologist and the historian but the main trends, as they affect the craft in Europe and America, must be understood to appreciate their silver. Techniques also evolved and spread, but they arose from the requirements of current style, which in turn, originated and developed through need, or an admiration of other art forms: the classical recurring most frequently throughout history. Design within a style largely stemmed from a common source, created either by groups working in proximity, as for example, within the protection of the Vatican, or the Louvre, or influenced by the books of patterns that were published and used by all.

It was rare for a piece of silver to be made entirely by the same hand, for although the fully trained craftsman was proficient in all branches of his trade, and so able to complete a work himself, he normally used specialists in such skills as engraving, casting or die cutting, whether retained by him or on a freelance basis. But he, the goldsmith, was responsible for any object that bore his mark. This was a personal device which, at first, was stamped upon a piece so that, should it later prove not to meet the metal standard required, the culprit would be known. Such marks were first punched in Rome during the 4th century, the craftsmen of most European countries forming themselves into guilds for the protection of their standards by the 12th or 13th centuries. Marks proving that an object was of the required standard followed as a logical consequence. They were necessary because silver and gold were alternative forms of currency, melted and used as such whenever money was required. This is the main reason why so little early silver survives.

Standards can vary because pure silver needs to be alloyed with another metal to make it sufficiently hard to be durable. The sterling standard of 925 parts silver to 75 of copper, was found to be satisfactory and was already in use in Britain in Saxon times. In the year 1300 Britain ordained its use and it was decreed that the mark of the leopard's head be stamped to show proof of its use by assay.

Silver was expensive; money perpetually in short

supply. The silver marking systems of the world have arisen through the natural desire to make the one go further in order to have more of the other, and authority's intent to prevent such debasement being practised. All marks were stamped to this end, whatever the standard adopted, usually sterling in early times. The officials who verified silver standards were elected for a limited period and, although the title given to the most important of them varied from country to country, date letters were used exclusively to show who was in charge when any object was assayed. This practice has proved convenient to the modern collector, but was *not* designed for his benefit. Town marks were necessary because every assay office had its own officials (even those unofficially maintained, such as Exeter or Barnstaple in England before 1700), while the standard mark proved the piece to have reached the requirements of that office. Later, in some countries, standards were lowered and in 1663 the Netherlands offered the choice of two standards, then three. With the exception of Britain, where no standard below sterling has ever been legal, reduction in standard (and in control in many countries) became fairly normal. All other marks appearing upon silver, wherever and whenever punched, also have a meaning, usually concerned with taxes.

Raising a beaker, German woodcut, 1480. The silver is hammered into shape over a piece of iron to keep it evenly distributed and frequently annealed in the furnace.

ITALY	ENGLAND	
c **380 AD** Marks first used in Rome	**1238** Standards set	Newcastle
1231 Regulations strictly enforced in Pisa, Siena & Florence	**1300** Leopard's head introduced to denote sterling standard	York
1358–98 Set standards for gold and silver	**1363** Maker's mark to be stamped after assay	**1720** Sterling standard & its marks resumed at the option the maker. New style town marks (1700) used whateve the standard
1508 Gold and Silversmith's Guilds separately organized	**1423** Seven provincial towns appointed to conduct their own assay. Newcastle Bristol York Salisbury Norwich Coventry Lincoln	
Rome adopts the mark of crossed keys	**1463** Annual date letter introduced, within the leopard's head	**1773** Birmingham and Sheffield appointed to assay silver
Genoa, a tower	**1478** Leopard's head crowned & separated from date. Three marks in all	**1784** Sovereign's head duty mark added
Naples. NAP or full name crowned	**1543** Lion passant standard mark adopted	**1821** Leopard's head mark r longer crowned
Turin, arms of the house of Savoy		**1890** Sovereign's head mark discontinued
Venice, winged lion of St Mark	**1697** Britannia standard introduced, to be assayed in London only. Denoted by figure of Brittania: lion's head erased; variable date letters and the maker's mark, now the 1st & 2nd letters of his surname	
1562 Standard set in Florence, where maker's mark obligatory. Rules changed from time to time		
1563 In Rome a maker's mark to be used in addition to the town mark	**1700** Five provincial towns appointed to assay silver of Britainia standard, adding the arms of the city to the 4 marks used in London: York, Exeter, Chester, Bristol, Norwich. Newcastle added in 1701	
1608–1811 Rome mark of crossed keys surmounted by an umbrella	Exeter	
c **1650–1720** Rome date marks stamped increasingly erractically	Chester	
1811 Italian marks conformed to the French		

THE MARKING OF SILVER IN EUROPE

GERMANY	FRANCE	SPAIN
13th cent. Maker's marks a device mentioned	**1275** An ordinance regarding town marks issued	**1298** Metal workers organized into a Guild
14th cent. Nuremburg and Augsburg strictly controlled	**1355** The above confirmed with maker's marks in Paris	**1401** Town stamp required throughout Spain
1516 Nuremburg adopts town mark: the letter N	**1472** Date letter introduced (obligatory 1506), continued until 1789, changing annually	**1492** Unification of Spain
1529 Augsburg adopts town mark: a pineapple	**1554** Standard of 95·8 per cent established. Initials added to the maker's device	
Pineapple varied with each warden until	**1672** Silver taxed, beginning the tax farmer system	
1735 date letter system introduced	**1677** Charge and discharge marks obligatory with wardens and maker's marks	
Not used after mid 19th cent.	28 town marks – each a letter – Paris an A, usually crowned	
1766 Nuremburg date letter system erratic till stopped mid 19th cent.	**1774** Tax farms abolished	
	1775 Same charge and discharge marks used throughout an area, all registered in Paris	
	1789 All supervision abolished. Virtual anarchy	
	1797 Maker's marks in a lozenge, but without fleur de lys. Single tax mark denoting 1st or 2nd class silver, 950/1000 or 800/1000	
	1817 Tax divided into 9 districts, each with its own symbol	
	1818 Annual marks introduced (still used)	
	1838 Single mark throughout France – still in use	

AN OUTLINE OF THE MAIN POINTS GOVERNIN

BELGIUM	SWEDEN	HOLLAND

BELGIUM

1355 Brussels adopts the lion rampant of Brabant as the town mark. Later crowned

1372 Maker's marks compulsory in Brussels

1400 Ghent standard mark

16th cent. Date letter

1502 Assayer's mark discontinued in Antwerp in favor of a yearly date letter. Little change in the system until Belgium occupied by France in 1794

Liège same rules as Antwerp but mark of a double headed eagle stamped on work already bearing the maker's mark

SWEDEN

1485 Maker's marks introduced in Sweden

1596 City arms to be stamped on all gold and silver

1689 A system of annually changing date letters introduced for Stockholm only

1690 All other cities establish their own date letter cycles at different dates from this time. Stamped beside the town arms.

Gothenburg

Stockholm

1752 A national mark of 3 crowns on a trefoil stamped to denote standard. Zigzag assay mark also scraped

1759–1926 Uniform date letter system to cover all Sweden & Finland using a series of 24 letters. The Roman capitals of each numbered – i.e. the first year of the 3rd cycle (1807) marked A3

1860 Arms to denote towns changed for letters. 150 of them using different letter styles and shield shapes

HOLLAND

Early 16th cent. Royal decree that all silver should b marked with annual date letter; maker's mark and the arms of the city. Zigzag assay groove scraped by the warde

Dordrecht 1608

Amsterdam 1657

1663 Above confirmed but with the choice of 2 standard

1690 Crowned provincial lio stamped to indicate standard of ·0934. City of Utrecht stamped its arms twice instea

Utrecht 1712

1798 Ancient Guilds disbanded. New assay marks in many places

1813 Practice of restamping any previously marked silver offered for sale causes a confusion of marks

1814 Date letters consistent throughout the country. Stamped with marks of town and maker. System still used. Marks later denoting the size of the object and the standarc used: ·0925, ·0833 or ·0800

1852 833 standard

SCOTLAND	RUSSIA	IRELAND
457 Marks of the maker and e deacon to be set on dinburgh silver	Town & date marks used early. Among the most important Moscow double headed eagle St Petersburg (Leningrad) 2 crossed anchors within a sceptre	**1498** Earliest mention of a Guild of goldsmiths in Dublin
485 Edinburgh town mark to e stamped between that of aker (1st) & the deacon 3rd) taken from the arms of e burgh		**1605** Marks referred to
		1637 Dublin marks effective – a harp crowned as standard and the maker Dublin
681 Date letter adopted in dinburgh : deacon's mark hanged to that of assay aster	**1613** Two trustees elected by merchants in Russian towns & all silver for sale marked showing town mark, date, and usually the maker	**1638** Date letter added in Dublin
	17th cent. Silver made for the church marked with a hand blessing, within an oval	**1729** A duty levied on Dublin silver (for the encouragement of tillage!) and shown by the figure of Hibernia from 1730. This has continued to be used and can be considered a Dublin town mark
536 Glasgow goldsmiths corporated with that of the ther hammermen		
681 The town mark of lasgow, a tree, fish and ell adopted, ogether with a ate letter system, ccasionally used ntil 1710, flanked y the maker's mark twice	**1722** Guilds organized and the names of all concerned recorded in every town. Continued until 1903	
	18th cent. Trustee's marks added, 3 letters within a heart	**1807** Sovereign's head duty mark in Dublin
	1896 Town marks discontinued	
759 Assay master's hark on Edinburgh ilver changed to hat of a thistle enoting standard	**20th cent.** Moscow & St Petersburg form a coalition	**NORWAY & DENMARK**
		1398–1818 Political union of Norway and Denmark with common laws governing silverwork
784 Sovereign's ead duty mark used n Edinburgh & lasgow		**1568** Bergen goldsmiths formed into a guild followed by Oslo and Trondheim with same rules
819 Assay office established n Glasgow using annual date etters : the lion rampant for tandard : the town and maker's mark		**Early-mid 18th cent.** Wardens appointed to ensure proper marking. Complete sets of town, maker, warden and date marks now found occasionally
890 Sovereign's head duty mark abandoned everywhere		

De Silversmit.   ·78

Hoe eel van stof,   Noch veel te grof.

Blanck Silver alte veel bemind,
    Van't Hert dat weerels is gesindt,
Ghy kund den honger niet versaaden,
    Der weldoorsiende en keurge Ziel,
    Wiens lust op uwen Oorspronckviel,
Om sich   met Ryckdom t'overlaaden.

A SHORT HISTORY OF WESTERN SILVER

Silver as a token of payment is known to have been used from about 4500 BC in ancient Babylon, since when its use both ornamental and practical has been fairly constant, epitomised in ancient Greece. By 2000 BC there were few techniques that had not been discovered, for the history of silver from that time is interspersed with familiar descriptions of embossing, engraving or casting, with flutes, gadroons or the chasing of mythological scenes, flowers and foliage. In 700 BC we read of "the old process of stamping ... in the new geometric style;" in the 4th century BC decoration in high relief was "revived." Nothing can be new, yet from an eight note octave or a 26-letter alphabet new music and literature have continued to pour, while the goldsmiths, often inspired by other art forms, have presented the skills handed down to them by the ancients, in ever new and lovely ways.

The Edict of Milan, which gave official recognition to Christianity in AD 313, was of prime importance to the history of silver in Europe, for the beautifying of the church then became the main task of the goldsmith for more than 1000 years. The most important influence at this time was Byzantium and the chief source of metal the melting down of vast quantities of plate from ancient Rome (fed by the spoils of Greece and Asia in the 2nd century BC). Silver was found and mined in small quantities in many places and used locally, often to great effect — as shown in Irish Celtic work, but needs were great and were otherwise met by plunder and trade with the east, and by Spanish mines, the main European source until new discoveries in Germany in about AD 900.

Very little work of this period survives, but magnificent silver was produced and often decorated with fine jewelry and enameling.

The gothic style

Between the 13th and 15th centuries French goldsmiths established general supremacy in both craftsmanship and design and France originated the style which later centuries have given the name of "gothic." From their beginnings in the churches of the Benedictine order at Vézelay and St Denis the new soaring building forms were echoed in the design of French silver and its influence quickly spread into Germany and other countries. The Italians took it to Spain and Portugal, where they worked in great

The goldsmith pours molten metal from a crucible, page from a Dutch book of 1704. The verse rebukes those who have too worldly a love of silver which cannot satisfy those who hunger for more spiritual things. The moralist seems lacking in the aesthetic appreciation which is so important to the silver collector.

numbers, Spanish goldsmiths producing accomplished raised statuary and Italian style enameling, which they used prolifically and in great variety. The gothic style, with its elegant cast spires, pointed arches, pinnacles, castellations and turrets, is so architectural that it is like the European cathedrals that reflect the same austere aspirations — enamels and jewels taking the place of stained glass windows. Most of the motifs used were those of the stonemason, the structure often overlaid with the most delicate tracery, while stamped moldings, well cast models of saints and other figures feature strongly, the figures also appearing as the finials on medieval spoons, or the lids of standing cups. Lombardic or gothic-style lettering may also be found, particularly on the ceremonial insignia of courts, guilds, colleges and cities which were also being furnished at the time.

The flowering of the renaissance

The 15th and 16th centuries were a period of fairly general political turbulence. Europe's finest goldsmiths flocked to Spain after its unification in 1492, when her mines were producing well and her extravagant aristocracy was requiring monumental silver for both church and home, but goldsmiths found working conditions at their best in Italy, under the Papal umbrella in Rome or the Medici in Florence, where art in every form was finding new expression. Wonderful architectural church plate was made there, color aided by gilding, lavish enameling and the use of varied metals, but with the atmosphere surging with creative excitement, new life and new form in silver and gold soon found expression and spread throughout Europe. Architects, medalists, painters, but above all sculptors, influenced the goldsmiths in this *renaissance* to blend the use of jewelry, enamels and glass in perfect harmony with lifelike figures in their compositions.

The renaissance introduced many motifs that have been used at times ever since, following the ancient classical lines of architecture, its figure modeling based on the great sculptures of the day, mostly human forms, but also animals, marine life or grotesques. Medallions were used, satyrs, nymphs, cherubs; swags of fruit, foliage, flowers and scrolls. Interlacing strapwork was important, often with matted grounds; caryatid or scroll brackets, flutes, acanthus leaves, pierced festoons of classical masks amid fleur de lys, flowers, anthemia or scrolls, and a variety of classically inspired

The Merode Cup, silver gilt, Burgundian, *c* 1400. Burgundy was particularly renowned for its enamels, here set in bands on both cup and cover. The arched panels, tracery and crocket embellishments all reflect gothic architectural styles.

Pair of silver gilt dishes, with central plaques of translucent enamel, Portuguese, late 15th century.

HISTORY

moldings, such as egg-and-dart, billet or ovolo. Michelangelo was among those to produce designs from which all could work and demand for church, civic needs and home was colossal.

But the style also traveled, Cellini himself taking it from Italy to Paris where he and other Italians worked at the court for some years, although scarcely anything survives because of almost continual religious wars. That the French adapted the Italian style to their own needs is known from their surviving designs for both domestic and church silver, and by the many French goldsmiths who found a more settled atmosphere abroad. The Germans were also of immense importance, for probably the greatest period in goldsmithing history began in Nuremburg and Augsburg early in the 16th century, with its emphasis on secular silver. Martin Luther had translated the Bible into German and reformed the church in 1530, so that the little made for the Lutheran church was simple, engraved or chased with sculptural scenes. The great goldsmiths of southern Germany, however, were superlative in every skill and their large drinking vessels, mounted shells or fantastic cups were magnificently executed, whether engraved, embossed or cast. Their sculptural models, particularly the human male, were perfect in every muscular detail and the stories they illustrated covered the subject broadly, using every available motif and technique. Standing cups were usually fantastic or grotesque, but those decorated with repoussé pineapple lobing, occasionally also found on tankards, were made only in Nuremberg, the distinctive lobes (or prickly bosses) of Portugal being rounder, in higher relief, stippled and more separate. Tankards were very large and usually showed biblical or allegorical subjects in strong embossing, while the beakers, deftly engraved with similar or sporting scenes, make for contrast in styles. Terrestrial globe cups also showed quality engraving, their bowls held up by the figure models, such as Atlas supporting the world. Double cups were another speciality, identical whichever way they stood and usually engraved, while fantastic animal or bird cups were also made only in southern Germany.

The international influence of this work was enormous, for patterns produced by German professional designers were used everywhere, often executed by first-class German goldsmiths who had migrated, many

Dutch Nautilus Cup with silver gilt mounts by Jan Jacobsz van Royesteyn of Utrecht, 1596.

HISTORY

of them to Antwerp which, owing to her maritime supremacy, was then culturally on a par with Rome and had very high standards of her own.

From that busy port skilled craftsmen spread out to Scandinavia, the Baltic and the Iberian peninsula. Spanish and Portuguese adventurers and explorers were opening up the world, colonizing it and bringing home gold and silver bullion, to Spain from South America in great bulk, to Portugal from Mexico, Peru and the east. Overall design in Portugal was wide and spacious, scrolling motifs standing out in open work, while in Spain, where design was always positive, all motifs were inclined to exaggeration. In Russia the east blended its influence with that of the renaissance, craftsmen of many nations there creating a distinctive style in which niello figured strongly.

Portugal, Germany and France all had an influence on English work and Hans Holbein, a close friend of Antwerp's greatest goldsmith, crossed the North Sea to design plate for King Henry VIII, who debased the coinage several times and took over the wealth of the monasteries he had dissolved in order to pay for his personal extravagance; the stamping of the lion passant from c 1543 was probably intended to show that the sterling standard for plate remained constant. Scandinavia (German influenced) and Holland traded briskly with eastern England and Scotland (totally separate at the time), both of whom gave refuge to European protestants, and the English, always more adaptive than inventive, absorbed all these various ideas, interpreting them to their own taste, and produced unmistakably English silver without originating a single motif. The English simplification of punch work came from Portugal, while stamped moldings and German strapwork, which became characteristic of English Elizabethan decoration, never could be mistaken for the originals.

English silver is relatively simple, for even the richly decorated Great Salt, which signifies the place of honor occupied by the nef on the French table, is light compared with continental embossed work of similar importance, on which few clear spaces are ever to be found. Crystal was still important in standing cups, for its supposed protection against poison, but enamels, dying out elsewhere, had disappeared totally from English work. A steeple surmounting a standing cup is distinctively English (from c 1590), as are the attractive

20

Silver gilt and crystal standing cup, English, 1573.

Pineapple standing cup, Nuremburg, c 1620.

HISTORY

flat-chased bell salts which, like contemporary flagons, feature stylized foliage and flowers within strapwork on a matted ground; similar strapwork in Italy or France would be in higher relief, with an exuberance of scrolls filled out with grotesque figures. Continental silver, in fact, increased in richness towards the end of the century, while England, always restrained, became more so, with attractive but light and occasionally beautiful work in the early 17th century, generally in formal floral patterns, giving way to plain silver of dull design under the Protectorate (except for the work of a few exceptional craftsmen). The reform of the church and the rise of Puritanism doubtlessly played their part, but although Queen Elizabeth I restored the currency to sterling standard, the country was slow to recover from the inflation Henry VIII had caused.

Antwerp was already losing her commercial position when the seven northern provinces were united at Utrecht in 1579, goldsmiths quickly following the transfer of power. The Netherlands had been slow to abandon the gothic style, extending the normal transitional period by incorporating certain renaissance features with it, such as repoussé mouldings or lion's masks in high relief.

The development of the baroque

With the world opening up from her thriving ports, art flourished in every form and goldsmiths broke away to work in their own naturalistic style to which the baroque form was admirably suited. This undisciplined style had gradually evolved in Italy during the renaissance and flourished alongside its forms, an irregularity of shape being one of baroque work's main

Embossed roundel, depicting Lot and his daughters, by Paul van Vianen, Dutch, 1604.

features, along with a complexity of design at times tantamount to abstract art in the grotesque oddity it displayed. The Italians had been inclined to overload work decorated in this way, but the south Germans were so exact in detail that the most heavily ornamented of their work never appeared cluttered. In Holland baroque was at first interpreted in an extraordinary, fluid and grotesque manner by Paul and Adam Van Vianen in the "cartilaginous" or lobed style they made famous — figures that did not always have a clearly defined outline blending rhythmically into the whole. Another Dutch form was the use of contrasting degrees of low relief to portray landscapes in silver, highlighted by surrounding grotesques and other strong renaissance motifs. Figural sculptures were retained for small

Dish, made with an accompanying ewer, illustrated on p. 61. They were commissioned by Genoese art patron Giacomo Lomellini and made by Italian craftsmen in 1619.

items for a while, but the Dutch rarely used casting, preferring embossing, at which they were very skilled, often creating a swirling movement that suggested a turbulent sea. Dolphins, above all other marine creatures, were a feature, as were grotesque masks that were neither quite man nor beast, while embossed cherubs' heads on the borders of dishes were also distinctive. This theme developed considerably so that by 1650 flowers, their continuous foliage entwining swags of fruit, animals and birds of every description were in very high relief, often with a dainty landscape in the centre of a dish. This style traveled the world, often executed by immigrant Dutch craftsmen, but was simplified in England where the motifs usually stand high individually on the very thin silver of porringers and their stands, rather than swirling into a composite whole.

The Portuguese, in their own more open way, were still making similar large dishes after 1700, but over-expansion and spending in Spain, together with a sharp decrease in bullion importation, had caused a serious recession in the peninsula early in the 17th century, when the court moved to Madrid. Nevertheless, until about 1665, silver in the grand manner was still made superbly, often with applied cabochons of lovely enamels and intricate filigree work. Germany, particularly Augsburg, continued in its own style; Scandinavian silver showing both German and French influence.

A Spanish Monstrance, *c* 1647.

The Dutch also brought the art of engraving to a peak never surpassed, particularly on octagonal dishes, their patterns and skilled craftsmen traveling the world, themselves creating the finest examples everywhere. The first New York craftsmen, *c* 1680, were Dutch and responsible for the high standard of engraving in that city, and for their own distinctive style thereafter. Exchange students between Aberdeen and Leyden universities first took the beautifully engraved Dutch beakers to Scotland. France, where native design was at a low ebb during the period of the Thirty Years' War, also benefited from the skill of these talented Dutch engravers.

World events at this time were changing the pattern of life. Silver was made in New England in Boston from about 1650, where the established church was not dissimilar to the Scottish kirk, requiring simple plate at first, serving both home and church needs until

Frame for a portrait,
Paris 1672, a
magnificent period
of French work from
which very little
survives.

HISTORY

Prints showing a goldsmith and his wife. They carry tools and equipment of their craft suspended from their belts and display a wide range of silverware in the latest styles: jugs, coffee pots, cups, trays, a sconce, candlestick and a mounted nautilus shell among those which can be identified. Augsburg, c 1730.

increasing prosperity brought greater skill and more elaborate requirements. Quebec, already settled by the French, had Catholic needs and followed French styles in high quality ecclesiastical work. Cromwell so overstated the virtues of piety that England was clamoring for cheerfulness as soon as Charles II returned to the throne from exile in 1660.

In 1661 Louis XIV of France came of age, married the Infanta Maria Theresa of Spain, and took over the reins of monarchy, for in the same year Cardinal Mazarin died, having guided Louis through his youth. Both kings had lavish ideas of living, so stimulating a great deal of work for goldsmiths (still in the Dutch style until c 1670, when France broke away). When Louis set about building Versailles he furnished it with quantities of furniture and fittings in solid silver, and his extravagant ways reflected through French society to

the more successful merchants, the poor largely having to bear the cost through increased taxation. The exodus of Huguenot goldsmiths from France went virtually unnoticed, but it was the most important event of the century in its effect on silver, reaching its culmination in the revocation of the Edict of Nantes in 1685, when more than a quarter of a million skilled craftsmen, including master goldsmiths, fled France and fanned out over Europe.

French goldsmiths, in the meantime, adapted the Dutch style to their own tightly scrolling form in much heavier silver, boldly sweeping, strongly embossed, often on a matted ground. Acanthus leaves, amorini with cast coiled snakes, applied cut card work and ornamental straps were used, workmanship being of the highest order, judging by the very little that survives. But extravagance had to be paid for and in

HISTORY

1672 a duty was imposed on plate, necessitating a third mark, punched by the tax farmer before completion of the work. The purpose of this mark was to discourage the conversion of silver into plate and the tax farmer was, by ancient practice, a man who bought the right to collect the taxes in his district, ensuring that he made a handsome profit on the transaction. A discharge mark, introduced in 1681, was stamped on finished work. Wars, too, required cash and by 1689, when virtually all the sumptuous plate of this superlative period was melted to pay military expenses, several lesser melts had already occurred, heralding in a more restrained period of goldsmithing.

In the meantime the melting pot in England cooled. Once again foreign craftsmen, including provincial Huguenots, arrived in the country, where goldsmiths were out of practice and standards were naturally low, although by the 1680s native goldsmiths such as the Garthornes and Anthony Nelme were creating lovely work in very varied styles, some of it in the finest French traditions, Dutch influence having ceased. A heavier gauge of metal was then being used, decorated with gadrooned edging, radiating acanthus leaves and vertical and spiral flutes, alternately concave and convex. Flat chased chinoiserie decoration was popular, all the work of one craftsman it is thought. It was not surprising that English goldsmiths objected to the influx of Huguenots after 1685 for they provided strong competition with their advanced skills and techniques, and their new forms such as helmet shaped

Painting by Richard Collins of a Family at Tea (detail). Note the cups without handles, the spoon tray and absence of a cream jug. c 1725.

jugs and harp handles. Their influence was enormous and English standards rose accordingly.

"Queen Anne" silver

In the new, carefree atmosphere of Restoration England everyone wanted silver and from vast wine cisterns for the nobility to tankards in the village pub, they had it. Bullion intended for the mint went to the goldsmiths, who also clipped coin or melted it for their own needs, so that the Exchequer suffered considerably. To overcome this problem a law was passed in March 1697 raising the standard of silver for plate to 95.8%, distinguishable from sterling (92.5%) by the marks of Britannia, the lion's head erased, a variable date letter and the first two letters of the maker's surname. This system operated in London only until 1700, when certain provincial offices were re-appointed to stamp their own silver.

Such soft silver was not suitable for elaboration, but fortunately a new simplicity had been introduced in France in about 1680, dependent upon line and quality rather than decoration, and this style was later used in virtually all countries, although not before 1700. Known in Britain and America as "Queen Anne" style, it met the needs of such soft silver. Silver in this style could be mistaken for the English "Queen Anne" wherever it was made. In fact, from that time, the silver of the western world began to lose its national characteristics and to evolve in common, with France leading the way. Differences, and of course they still existed, became more a matter of degree than of

The Newdigate centerpiece, by Paul de Lamerie, London, 1743. Of Dutch birth, Lamerie was taken to England as a baby and became one of London's leading silverworkers.

HISTORY

fundamentals — and of date. England's Queen Anne reigned from 1702–1714, yet the elegant silver that bears her name was made until 1730 in England, increasing in ornament after 1720, when the sterling standard was restored; until c 1770 in Italy, owing to the withdrawal of Papal and Medici support, and from c 1720–50 in America. The Queen's reign, in fact, had little to do with the style (and the term "Georgian silver" is even less descriptive, for that period stretched from 1714–1830, embracing many styles). Britannia standard silver, with its rich patina, was contributory to the excellence of British silver, with its unsurpassed beauty of line and fine quality engraving, now superior to the French. Essentially this was silver in tapering cylindrical, spherical or baluster form, often polygonal and with lovely facets, particularly on candlesticks. Cut card work, horizontal mouldings or simple vertical straps were used, as were gadrooned borders (mainly on tankards), good armorial engraving, simple moldings and domed covers but flutes and matted backgrounds were more prevalent on the Continent.

Peter the Great westernized the Russian silver industry when he moved his capital to St Petersburg in 1700, importing foreign goldsmiths, largely German and Swedish, adopting their styles and instituting a hallmarking system. Germany, with Augsburg preeminent, had come under French influence in about 1700, making many of the same objects, but adapting them to her own taste, incorporating inset coins, restrained chasing filled in by matted backgrounds and lovely figural handles to otherwise plain tankards. Scandinavia, while accepting some French shapes and a little of their simplicity, particularly for candlesticks, still retained much that was baroque and old German.

Régence and rococo

The Régence style in France (Louis XIV died in 1715 when his great grandson, Louis XV, was a minor) developed from c 1700, maintaining shapes but increasing ornament in flat chasing with fine interlacing and continuous tapering straps, curved and straight; guilloche borders; symmetrical scrolls alternating with foliate forms, medallions and other classical motifs, mostly on matted grounds, which make a great difference to overall appearance. Standards were high with a brilliant finish and it was not long before the asymmetrical rococo style developed from it.

One of a pair of beer jugs by Phillips Garden, London, 1754. Covered jugs for beer are not usual at this date but the decoration featuring a barrel and ears of barley are an indication of purpose.

HISTORY

With few exceptions (and there always were exceptions) English silver adopted such ornament cautiously and never completely, continuing with simple, elegant silver until *c* 1730, although engraving gave way to flat chasing in Huguenot hands, and some Régence motifs, such as shells and scrolls, were used increasingly. By that time French rococo was building up towards its fantastic peak, but the English, taking their first tentative steps in this asymmetrical form in about 1730 were always more restrained. Exuberant rococo was understood by few and the form was frequently misinterpreted by lesser craftsmen, even in France, for abstract scrolls could swirl pointlessly while naturalistic "rocaille" with its fishes, crustacea and other marine creatures, shells and pebbles, flowers, fruits and foliage, occasionally swirling round the human body, could degenerate into meaningless jumbles. At best this apparently lawless work was imaginative, amusing and perfectly balanced, cast in heavy silver in very varied texture. The period was comparatively peaceful, even the middle classes buying domestic plate, while the nobility and crowned heads of Europe, for whom magnificent dinner services were made, were lavish in their demands. Those foreign orders were almost all that survived the French Revolution.

In a goldsmith's workshop, Paris, 1771, showing work in several processes.

The rococo style, liable to exaggeration with heavy detail swamping the flowing movement of the little made in countries such as Spain and Germany, was nevertheless also dependent on many basic forms that were used everywhere. These included such items as the double scroll handle, almost universal by 1740, swan-neck spouts for tea and coffee pots, with swirling cast scrolls supporting them; pear-shaped bodies, giving way to the inverted pear by mid century; cast snake handles, coiling sinuously; scroll and shell borders to salvers (sometimes described as "piecrust"); swing handles and pierced scroll or diaper patterns for baskets and, above all, superlative armorial engravings within asymmetrical cartouches.

In America, where Philadelphia's Joseph Richardson was among the few to attempt much rococo decoration (delightfully, for his interpretation was not overcrowded), these factors were used throughout the period (*c* 1740–80) with little if any ornament. Rococo embellishment was also rare in Scandinavia, (*c* 1750–75) and then was often overstated, Christian

A page of designs for ewers, wine jugs, bell, sprinkler, holy-water vessel and a tray to hold them for the Mass, Paris, 1771. Note the base designs.

HISTORY

Precht of Stockholm being one exception, with some beautiful work. English interpretation of the decorative form was mainly good, particularly by the London Huguenots whose workmanship was excellent and engraving outstanding. Some English rococo was very imaginative and, if few attempted the excesses delighted in by Charles Kandler or Nicholas Spirmont, a great deal was fully ornamented with a combination of strength, delicacy and balance, shown to perfection by Paul de Lamerie. Chinese decoration, used little elsewhere, became a rage in England in about 1745 and Chinese rococo scenes, sometimes excessive and tasteless, particularly in the pagoda form, might be embossed on any suitable surface, used as figural finials or as superbly modeled candlesticks. Ireland, who had followed English styles closely in superlative quality, also copied these Chinese styles but by 1750 had developed her own most distinctive form of rococo decoration, interpreting nature in her own way with birds amid the flowers and foliage, fish and fishermen, cows and milkmaids, dogs, sheep and cottages amid the trees — the Irish country scene in fact, at best on their distinctive dish rings, but sometimes offset on a sauceboat by a formal handle such as a dolphin, its tail twisting typically.

Drastic changes in the social climate were creating new classes of customer for goldsmiths almost everywhere, and the discovery of the process known as Sheffield Plate in 1742 was of far reaching significance. This method of fusing silver sheet on to copper was comparatively unimportant for another twenty years, but its evolution, the discovery of vast new sources of Mexican bullion in 1759 and the increasing use of machines all helped to reduce prices progressively and to make silver available to people unable to afford expensive rococo.

Neo-classicism

Change was in the air and when foreign travel became fashionable during the 1750s, with emphasis on the antiquities of Greece and Rome, the new classical era began in France, its decoration at first used on the familiar curved shapes. Most French silver in this style was lost in 1789 however, when the ancient guild system was abolished and all supervision ceased for six years.

The Revolution punctuated the story of French goldsmithing but was no full stop, for after six bleak

Neo-classic style chocolate pot with beaded edges and chased and repoussé decoration, English, 1773–4.

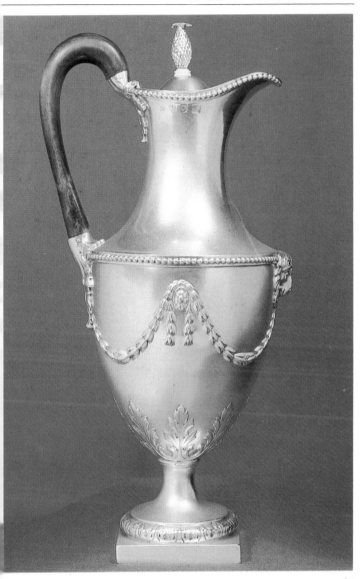

HISTORY

years, when the goldsmiths' guilds had been disbanded and all supervision ceased, they picked up the tools of their trade and carried on creating fine silver. The fully classical Empire style evolved quickly from this time, and there was no shortage of work, for Napoleon and his friends gave them huge orders, including vast gifts to foreign courts, mostly gilded. This work was considerably aided by power and machine techniques. The craft was re-organized in 1797, with marks, which

Quart cann by Paul Revere, Boston, showing his unmistakable mark, c 1780.

had been regional, becoming common throughout France(although few outside Paris retained importance). They consisted of maker's initials and a device (other than a crowned fleur de lys) within a lozenge; a single, somewhat variable mark, replacing those for charge and discharge and the figures 1 or 2, denoting a standard of 95% or 80% — most countries other than England having by then adopted standards below sterling for unimportant work. French mark styles were basically copied by countries the French had formerly overrun but, although further changes took place in 1819 and 1838, marking throughout continental Europe had become too lax to be reliable.

By 1770 most of Europe had followed the French classical style for elliptical or narrow necked vase-shaped objects, with regular, rational decoration in all the old motifs, such as ram's heads, masks, flower or laurel wreath festoons and ribbons, acanthus and other formal foliage; patterae, medallions, hoops, shallow flutes, lobes and gadroons. Engraving, other than for armorials, was rare, but piercing began to appear and after the Revolution strong embossing or cast and applied work and more grandiose designs became the rule. These were heavily laden with winged sphinxes, griffins, snakes, Medusa heads and other Egyptian or mythological figures, frequently used as handles or feet, with the Imperial eagle as a finial until 1815. Italy, very formally classical, was considerably more restrained, and after 1815 France also continued the form without the wealth of decoration, stamped borders and perhaps a medallion or simple mythological application sufficing on the plain, burnished surfaces, with handles or spouts, still cast in classical forms, enhanced by the surrounding simplicity.

In England Robert Adam's name became synonymous with the period and in the early, formal stage (1770–80) his designs, and those copying his architectural lead, were of paramount importance. The ruins that had inspired him in Greece and Rome were of pure, elegant line, uncluttered by extraneous matter, and the houses he planned, complete with their interior decoration and contents, were modeled upon those ruins, although some of his contemporaries were less exact. On silver classical columns, usually on a square, gadrooned base, urns and combinations of straight lines with symmetrical curves were used in the most balanced manner, decorated with formal borders,

HISTORY

festoons, medallions, patterae, shallow fluting and beading, with high loop handles, occasionally in snake form and ram's head masks supporting ring handles.

This silver was comparatively light by continental standards, but became more so in every sense by 1780 when the new rich of England forced enterprising goldsmiths to new tactics by disdaining hand craftsmanship, preferring Sheffield plate which looked like silver and could be had at a fraction of the cost. By then machines were rolling silver ever thinner and, after Matthew Boulton had obtained the right for Birmingham and Sheffield to assay their own plate in 1773, these goldsmiths quickly entered the cut-price war, using the same machines as the platers, very thinly rolled silver and simple designs suitable to these techniques. Line continued on the oval plan, with the narrow necked urn shape for tall objects, virtually without decoration after 1780, except when machine stamped. The drop stamp revolutionized production and was largely used for making wine labels, caddy spoons or hollow-ware sections in Birmingham (which punched its work with an anchor). In Sheffield (using a crown mark) the process was used to turn out parts for candlesticks complete with decoration that was so sharp that no hand improving was needed. These parts were then soldered together in any permutation and filled with a hardening agent for support (loaded). No firm had a monopoly on any candlestick design and patterns, whether in fused plate or silver, while unmistakably Sheffield, cannot be further distinguished.

The fly punch produced simple, geometric, pierced patterns in quantity and was used for containers with blue glass liners, such as baskets, salts, mustard pots and sugar basins, or the surrounds of objects such as decanter or ink stands. Wire was machine-drawn to any thickness and to any pattern, including twisted rope, beading or reeding and could be used for handles, rims, edging or a complete basket. Such machines led to a certain sameness, yet their very restrictions were responsible for an elegance previously unknown. Nevertheless, it would be as wrong to assume that no hand work emanated from Birmingham and Sheffield, however rare, as that London goldsmiths did not also avail themselves of these commercial short cuts on many occasions.

By 1780 silver in this graceful style was the rule and

Coffee pot and vase by Abraham Dubois, Philadelphia, c 1770. Note the typical bold pineapple finial and extra small beading (see p. 40).

was usually decorated only with shallow flutes and beading before bright-cut engraving came in during the 1780s, to add its sparkling finish to almost all work, picking out the lightest of classical floral festoons, ribbons and foliage with its burnishing graver, sometimes in between the cuts of pierced silver, transforming its regular appearance, while broad flutes and shaped edges also added interest.

The style did not prevail, for massiveness was deemed preferable to elegance from the start of the 19th century, and by 1810, when France was embarking on a long period of restrained classical taste, England had entered her last formal, recognizeable period, before losing all semblance of discrimination. In

HISTORY

Germany, where classical influence had been confined to the application of festoons, occasional medallions and beaded borders, the universal fall from standards arrived soon after 1800 when lighter metal became general. Any suggestion of classicism then disappeared and ornate lack of taste prevailed. Italian silver maintained classical ornament in a restrained manner and was not dissimilar from the later French style, with spouts and handles the main points of interest, but, until after 1780, Scandinavia retained curved rococo shapes to which they applied festoons of laurel and other classical motifs in their own way. The urn shape, broader than elsewhere as a variable rule and raised on a footed, sometimes gadrooned square plinth, appeared late in the 1790s, but the French Empire style was adapted to their taste between 1810–30, when eclecticism of a comparatively restrained form set in.

Scottish work had by this time become indistinguishable from the English, ancient barriers having been broken down, but Irish silver, while adopting the English neo-classic line, still had an indefinably Irish appearance, even though romanticism appeared only occasionally among the dainty motifs. Machines were not used in Ireland and true Irish silver lacks the mechanical precision and sameness, so apparent in plate assembled in Ireland from imported pre-fabricated parts, which nevertheless bear Irish marks. Slight variations in proportion may also be noted, such as the height of Irish boat-shaped sugar baskets, while dish rings, now hand-pierced in geometric designs, the beauty of their soup ladles and, although copied in America, the pointed ends of Irish spoons of the period are also distinctive features. Union with England in 1800 unfortunately killed independent design and Irish goldsmiths thereafter merely copied English patterns or assembled the English factory-made parts.

Because of the effects of the American Revolution (War of Independence), little silver was made in the newly-united States during the 1780s and in Boston, where feelings and action had run particularly high, virtually only Paul Revere was of importance until England, involved with France, relaxed trade restrictions and allowed prosperity to return to their former colony. The English style of neo-classicism was then taken up wholeheartedly, initials within cartouches replacing the armorials previously used and now considered too English. In American hands the tall, narrow-necked urn form was distinctively concave or spool-shaped, covers reflecting this movement in stately elegance, particularly noticeable on Philadelphian work, where extra height added to the effect. By this time any real individualism was almost universally a thing of the past, but Philadelphia, more active during the 1780s than was possible further north, quickly established an unmistakable style of its own. This included a particularly bold pineapple finial, beading, which in this city was smaller than elsewhere and applied to virtually all edges, and the characteristic pierced gallery, used nowhere else, which stands on the shoulders of some of their urn-shaped objects, such as coffee pots and covered sugar urns, made in the US in preference to baskets until about 1800. Although tankards were made, with a higher domed cover and foot than elsewhere and a distinguishing open-work thumbpiece, it was the tea table that dominated silver work during this period, bright cut-engraving (particularly fine in New York) enhancing the broad flutes to which American goldsmiths were partial, particularly in Boston.

Inkstand by Paul Storr, London, 1812, with silver-mounted glass bottles, on a fine quality silver tray.

HISTORY

Nineteenth-century flamboyance and decline

The War of 1812, when England was so tactless as to burn the city of Washington, caused a major break with tradition. American designers generally adopted the French Empire style from that time and, although they moved eventually into their own form of 19th-century eclecticism, they never embarked on the English Regency style which was massive and formal, but great at its best, in technique, workmanship and design. At first the change was gradual, with either Roman or Greek motifs on much more substantial silver of classical shapes, and although bright-cut engraving and ever lessening Greek elegance persisted until about 1810, heavier styles, partly adapted but not copied from the French, then took over, the Roman trend becoming ever stronger. This was a grand period everywhere, when industry flourished and men thought big, and bullion, mostly from Mexico and the US, was in plentiful supply. After victories such as Waterloo Englishmen felt big themselves and required all around them to conform in size, with every motif positive, whether heavily embossed or cast. In England this included vine leaves, grapes and all the bacchanalian scene (not used in France), familiar classical motifs from every period, winged sphinxes, inspired originally by French victories in Egypt, and classical figures which became increasingly sculptured. Already the form was too complex for designers lacking in classical understanding and it became more so when the greater talents also incorporated rococo, baroque and other trends into the mixture, somehow ending with a balanced design, quite beyond average ability. This contributed towards the decline in standards, complete soon after 1820, for so much plate was required by the new rich that all classes of goldsmiths were kept busy. Large impersonal firms, run as commercial businesses, had by then largely taken over from the individual goldsmith, some of them employing hundreds of men in addition to absorbing the whole output of smaller firms, whose mark they overpunched. The king, George IV, commissioned enormous quantities of plate for the royal household, but silver was mostly now made for the shop window, the newly revived technique of spinning for hollow-ware cutting costs considerably. A continual stream of new rich required domestic wares, and Sheffield plate was able to supply them flamboyantly and well, but the greatest demand was for

Victorian 5-light centerpiece by E. J. and W. Barnard, London, 1849. A glass dish in a bacchanalian holder surmounts a very typically sculptural design, made as a presentation piece.

HISTORY

London made bowl,
1907, showing
hammer marks.

presentation plate and trophies, including enormous centerpieces which told the whole story of some event in sculptured silver. Firms therefore employed sculptors as their chief designers, men who knew nothing of the demands peculiar to silversmithing, so that the techniques of the craft were forgotten. Detail was crammed on to every object, without regard to design, and the tasteless muddle that resulted from an uneducated mixture of styles won the day so completely that even lovely antique silver was refashioned to conform with it.

The use of thin silver, unsuitable to the massive style, was no longer an aid to those whose prestige depended on a large display of plate, but this problem was solved when Elkington and Company, of Birmingham, England, patented an electro-plating process in 1840. This revolutionized the craft and killed Sheffield plating, for with it pure silver was applied by electrolysis to articles which had been mass-produced in the cheap base metal known as German silver, giving a realistic yet factory-made appearance, the desired effect of which all were so proud. Electrotyping, which developed concurrently, cut costs further by removing totally the need for craftsmanship: for any article could now be reproduced in perfect detail, however intricate and whatever the original material, without effort or skill. Thus growing flowers or leaves were typeset and naturalism was added to the melée of design.

The story of decline followed a similar pattern almost everywhere and as the status of the goldsmith disappeared, so did concern for standards, which were now mostly two-tiered and not enforced; for example it

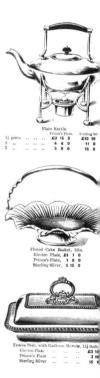

Plain Kettle.

	Prince's Plate.	Sterling Sil
1½ pints	£3 15 0	£10 10
2 ,,	4 4 0	11 0
3 ,,	5 0 0	16 0

Fluted Cake Basket, 10in.
Electro Plate, £1 1 0
Prince's Plate, 1 8 0
Sterling Silver, 5 15 0

Entrée Dish, with Gadroon Mounts, 11½ inch

Electro Plate	..	..	£2 18
Prince's Plate	..	..	3 16
Sterling Silver	..	..	15 6

44

English, advertisement, early 20th century, many of the pieces reflecting the eclectic reproduction styles then common, although the straight-forward cigar and cigarette box owes nothing to earlier periods.

was not illegal to sell plate below the statutory 80% in Germany, where marking was optional, while in France, although unlawful to sell silver at home under the standards of 95% or 80%, it was permissible to do so for export. Britain alone never fell below the sterling standard and maintained strict hallmarking supervision. In the US, where no assay system had ever been considered necessary, standards were adhered to voluntarily. Some American silver was stamped with the word "standard" during the 1830s, indicating 89.2% of silver, as used in coin at the time, the words "pure coin" indicating 90% after 1837, with "coin" as before, sometimes shown as "D" and "C" respectively after 1850 – the word "sterling" was used to indicate that standard only after 1860.

HISTORY

During the 19th century art schools and exhibitions proliferated and so did revival styles. Those designers who mixed the features of rococo, renaissance or any other period at random (often employing electrotyping or even plating), defeated the intended purpose of reviving craftsmanship. Materials were also mixed, particularly in the gothic revival which incorporated various metals (as the Italians and others had done in the past) with enamels and semi-precious stones and all the old gothic motifs in pure form. This more important revival persisted throughout the century from about 1830 and produced Roman Catholic church plate over most of Europe, without necessarily copying old pieces blindly; nevertheless, when applied to domestic plate it failed miserably, for nothing could be more incongruous than a pinnacled teapot.

Because travel and communications were easy, trends were fairly universal and even protestant Holland produced gothic plate for the Catholic Church. Yet in Russia, which had largely broken away from the European influences which had dominated them for so long, the general trend was towards old Russia and the East, with nielloed work reminiscent of Byzantium, boldly designed and carefully executed at best. The name Carl Fabergé stands out, but in this, their greatest period, he was not alone in such quality workmanship. Fabergé was not primarily concerned with silver but in any medium a large part of his personal success lay in the richness of his work, for he catered exclusively for the very wealthy. He also revived an old Russian

Mug by Omar Ramsden, London, 1921.

custom of giving eggs within the family at Easter, and his first jeweled egg, produced in 1868, was a success that echoed in orders from around the world.

The Arts and Crafts Movement

Reaction to lack of craftsmanship was inevitable and took several forms over the next 50 years, all planned as a direct revolt against mass-production. The Arts and Crafts Movement was begun in England in about 1875, and quickly spread all over Europe and America in varying forms, creating silver that was not only hand-made, but was necessarily seen to be so. In England this deliberately accentuated the lack of training and proficiency of the early craftsmen. Design was simple, good and new, but undoubtedly at first workmanship was crude with hammer marks left unpolished, rivets used openly and stones inset in the roughest manner, particularly in the workshops of C. R. Ashbee who made

21-light candle holder by Stuart Devlin, London, 1974, typical for its slim elegance; tracery and textured surface.

HISTORY

an attraction of incompetence and untrained labor. Some aspects of Art Nouveau, as practised in England's restrained manner, incorporated these same features, and indeed were occasionally designed by the same men, although the pioneers were totally opposed to it.

Art Nouveau

Art Nouveau began on the Continent in about 1890 and developed from the naturalism which, in some places, had never totally died. This was taken up enthusiastically all over Europe and the US (where New York now led in every way), and particularly in Spain and Belgium. At best it had a swirling grace and was not overstated, especially in the slim vase form so typical of Tiffany and Company of New York, sometimes with silver flowers overlaid on glass. Shape, however, was no defined part of the style, which concerned itself with flowing design, from the wind in a girl's hair to the sinuous movement of climbing plants: poppy, lily or honesty, their stems and foliage curving supinely in the typical whiplash form, which was altogether stronger and less graceful in England where most people were too self-conscious for success in this medium.

The twentieth century

Art Deco, started in France in about 1910, was never a real force in silver, and, although it spread widely, the best of it was largely French made. Its chunky, often cubist or abstract form, sometimes incorporated designs taken from primitive countries, while other pieces remained totally undecorated. It was a total breakaway from art nouveau and the functional style, so popular in Sweden from that time on, may be seen in some of its more practical pieces. It cleared the way for that to follow. Design and line always had been good in Sweden and the purely functional style of their modern work gained immense general popularity after 1945, until interest was restored to silver by textured surfaces, beauty and first-class workmanship. During the 1970s art was restored to the ancient craft of the goldsmith, now at its highest peak for two hundred years, craftsmen creating new designs for a once-only commissioned order and executing them by hand. Such silver is no longer purely functional but the best has the avowed intention of beautifying and enriching life even when it is a piece intended for use.

The spread of silver style through Europe and the movement of silver workers. These maps give a general picture for each of the main stylistic periods while the chart overleaf shows the position in the main silver-producing countries.

48

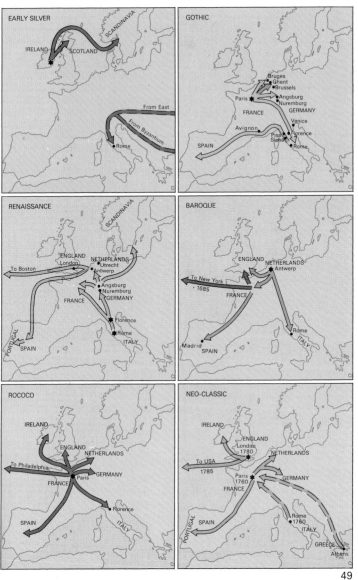

EARLY SILVER

IRELAND · SCOTLAND · SCANDINAVIA

From East
From Byzantium
Rome

GOTHIC

Bruges
Ghent
Brussels
Paris · Angsburg · Nuremburg
FRANCE · GERMANY
Venice
Avignon · Florence
Pisa · Siena
SPAIN · Rome

RENAISSANCE

SCANDINAVIA
ENGLAND · NETHERLANDS
London · Utrecht · Antwerp
To Boston
Angsburg · Nuremburg
FRANCE · GERMANY
Florence
Rome
PORTUGAL · ITALY
SPAIN

BAROQUE

ENGLAND · NETHERLANDS · Antwerp
To New York · 1685
FRANCE
Rome
Madrid · ITALY
SPAIN

ROCOCO

IRELAND
ENGLAND · NETHERLANDS
To Philadelphia · Paris · GERMANY
FRANCE
Florence
SPAIN · ITALY

NEO-CLASSIC

IRELAND
ENGLAND · NETHERLANDS
London · 1780
To USA · Paris · GERMANY
1785 · 1760
FRANCE
Rome · 1760
PORTUGAL · ITALY
SPAIN · GREECE
Athens

49

THE SPREAD OF STYLES AND CRAFTSMEN

	SPAIN AND PORTUGAL	NETHERLANDS	GERMANY
Early Silver			Aachen (Charlemagne's capital) attracts foreign goldsmiths.
Gothic	c 1400 Portuguese navigators bring great riches. 1492 Columbus discovers America Spanish style develops from I Italian. Superb enamelling.	Late 14th century: craftsmen from France settle in Bruges, Brussels, Ghent and Antwerp.	Late 14th century: Nuremberg and Augsburg earn very high reputation with gothic silver and reach heights with renaissance work.
Renaissance	Portugal excels with a mixture of gothic and renaissance c 1500	Flanders goldsmiths thrive with Antwerp rivalling Rome as center of art. Utrecht important.	German influence radiates over Europe. Church silver remains gothic until late 16th century.
Baroque	In Madrid craftsmen from many countries produce great silver for the court in a mixture of renaissance and baroque.	Baroque emerges in Netherlands and dominates Europe. 17th century the greatest period of Dutch craftsmanship. At end of century Dutch influence fades.	1614–48 Thirty Years War. German heavy baroque style.
"Queen Anne"	Portugal: English style with Indian motifs.		Germany's first almost plain period.
Rococo	French rococo imposed on Portugal's own rich style.		Over-elaboration of French style.
Neo-classical			Individual interpretation of neo-classical.
Modern	Some art nouveau	Art nouveau.	

FRANCE	ITALY	BRITISH ISLES	AMERICA
	AD 313 Edict of Milan. Rome is the capital of Christendom. Early Christian silver influenced by Byzantium and the east.	Magnificent Celtic work in Ireland. Vikings plunder Irish silver, leaving some in Scotland on the way home.	
Gothic starts in French monasteries. Supreme in 13th and 14th centuries. Unrest leads to migrations to Flanders.	Venice, Pisa, Siena Florence and Rome, centers of Italian gothic.	1066–1555: Close cultural ties with France.	
Renaissance influence from Italy c 1525. Continued emigration to Flanders and England.	Renaissance develops in Rome and Florence and spreads to France and Germany.	c 1535: Renaissance reaches England from Germany, Flanders and France.	
France leading with superlative silver (mostly lost 1688 to pay for wars). 1685: Revocation of Edict of Nantes: Huguenot craftsmen flee, spreading over Europe and America, and especially to England and the Netherlands.	Exuberant baroque.	1642–49: Civil War, "economy" silver in puritan England. Baroque style from Netherlands and France after return of monarchy in 1660.	1620: First pilgrim settlers reach New England. c 1640 First goldsmith established in Boston. Dutch inspired silver being made in New York (New Amsterdam).
Rococo develops from Regence in France and reaches its peak before 1730 when its influence begins to spread across Europe.	Plain "Queen Anne" until 1770, side by side with fine baroque. Italian rococo restrained.	"Queen Anne" style as originated in France, superlatively made in Britannia standard silver, c 1700–20 Rococo developing from 1730. Irish distinctive.	c 1690: Goldsmiths established in Philadelphia. American rococo restrained—at its best in Philadelphia. c 1785: The "Federal" style.
Classical revival begins during 1750s becoming the Empire style c 1780, plain and elevant to 1850.	1760: Classical revival begins in Rome; 1770 elsewhere.	c 1765–80 Classical revival. c 1780–1800: English form of neo-classicism developing. c 1800–30: "Regency" style. 1875: Arts and crafts movement.	c 1815–40: French Empire style. 1861–65: Civil War (most southern silver lost). English styles.
Art nouveau.	A little art nouveau.	Art nouveau.	Art nouveau. Tiffany.

APPRECIATING SILVER

APPRECIATING SILVER

Few silver collectors today can afford to make a purchase in error, for the outlay involved prohibits tossing aside a piece that fails to please in order to buy something new. Every object bought should be right in itself and meaningful to its owner, stimulating interest in its history, workmanship, marks and beauty, whether it is a marvellous example of antiquity or a comparatively modern trinket. The best way to acquire real understanding of the subject is to handle silver regularly, but this is often impossible for the small collector. Looking at the finest quality work objectively is also an education, for if the eye is constantly filled with things as they should be it will readily reject that which is wrong. The full value of museum collections is not always realized, for although much that is oldest and best will be found in them, set out to stimulate the greatest interest and delight, many also house specialist collections of objects that are not necessarily either particularly old or magnificent. It is just as valuable for the small collector to see the best hand-raised wine labels alongside those which were die-stamped, as it is for another to study the particular traits of the immigrant Huguenot goldsmiths.

Quality is a somewhat enigmatic asset, comprising perfect balance, weight, patina, understanding of a style and workmanship within it. Perfection is rarely found but, like the excellent, will have suffered neither damage nor alteration, will have original decoration and armorial engraving and will be punched with the full set of marks then in use, correctly grouped and spaced. Such silver will always hold its value and, in good times, increase it.

Patina is an almost infallible guide to original condition, for it is a deep skin, created by care, old age and an oxide on the surface which, like any other perfect complexion, should be glowing and unblemished. A break in the surface of this skin is discernible when any repair or alteration has been made, however well executed, and when looking for flaws the condition of the patina is the first consideration. This is less easy to detect on silver that is decorated overall than on a plain surface, but the metal of one piece is rarely of exactly the same color and condition as that of another. The erasure of armorials makes for a thin area of shiny silver, easily discernible in the patina, as is the insertion of a patch, the line of which also becomes visible when tarnished or breathed upon, whether the intention was to transpose armorials or repair damage. Decoration has frequently been placed over this line to hide it.

Such a patch line surrounding hallmarks would, however indicate the possibility of fraudulent practice, for the cutting out of good marks from a broken piece and soldering them into a new body is, and was, a favorite deceit, practised with cunning skill. Because age bestowed no additional value, the aim of the British forger, until comparatively recently, was not so much to deceive the customer as to avoid the expense of hallmarking or the payment of duty. This "duty-dodging" was done mainly in the periods 1719–59 and 1784–1890, when a duty was imposed on English silver by weight, shown during the later periods by the mark of the sovereign's head. The work of craftsmen avoiding this tax was often up to their own best standards and generally entailed the use of contemporary marks punched on small objects such as watch cases or saucers, which they had assayed before inserting them into the base of a large object, or the stem of a spoon might be used as a footwire. Such deceptions usually employed contemporary silver.

Pair of candlesticks by Paul de Lamerie, London, 1732, partly facetted and octagonal, with a sunken base.

APPRECIATING SILVER

Fakes and forgeries

The intent of the modern swindler, often using similar methods, is to raise the apparent value of worthless silver, presenting it to the buyer as antique. His work, often made from sub-standard metal, may be electrotyped from a genuine object of the required period and treated to look old, the marks transposed as described or taken from a small portion of a genuine but broken off piece, such as the neck of a jug, that fits the fraudulent object without unnatural joins.

The soldering together of broken parts of various ancient spoons is another modern fraud, either bringing together Apostle or other early finials with any suitable old stem, or faking marks on reproduction stems. The conversion of 18th-century spoons to become forks of similar period was also practised because of their greater rarity value. Faked marks, although rare, are mostly punched on modern frauds but may be detected: a home-made brass punch by its soft outline, a casting, placed identically on all pieces, by a fuzzy texture, or electrotyping by technical aids. Occasionally the less skilled forger used electroplating to give a uniform appearance to a made-up object, but this gives a patina inconsistent with supposed age and, in any case, is too easily detected to be effective.

Such forgers, unlike the duty dodgers, were frequently ignorant of the complex subject with which they were tampering and therefore made dire mistakes, both in the composition of old spoons (when many variables, such as bowl shapes, had to be understood for the fraud to be effective) and the correct placing and grouping of hallmarks. This enormous subject varies from country to country and with time, and when any doubt arises as to the genuineness of an object, or its marks, a specialist book on the subject should be consulted. For a broad rule of thumb, marks should move with the line of the piece on which they are struck; those beneath a round object such as a teapot (always marked underneath in England until the 19th century) should be grouped in the center, never in a straight line as they would be, for instance, on the basewire of a candlestick. Another invariable point in English silver is that each and every separable part of any piece should be individually marked.

It is also illegal in Britain to add to a piece of hallmarked silver or to alter its character, unless such additions amount to no more than $\frac{1}{3}$ the original

A Silver fork with the hallmarks for 1776 (see detail, *right*) on the handle, but with prongs substituted for the original spoon bowl. Forks were rare at the time and so of greater value to the forger.

A Victorian ewer in the style of 1765 bearing genuine marks of that date let into the body in the ovoid panel below the rim and to the right of the handle.

weight, when they must be separately hallmarked. This includes spouts, handles or replacement lids to objects such as teapots, a point to be watched by the buyer, for new marks reduce value. Major alterations, completely transforming a piece, chiefly the work of unscrupulous makers who considered one object more commercial than another, were illegal unless the old marks (which they preferred to keep) were totally erased. Nevertheless, fakes and forgeries are rare, for the expert usually notices any discrepancy and suspect English articles can be tested, on request, by a special committee at Goldsmiths' Hall. Genuine duty dodging marks appear in a somewhat different light, for they may be found on silver of superlative quality, as illustrated by the tea kettle by Joseph Ward, 1719 (p. 2); this weighs 85 ozs and would have been costly in duty if offered for assay.

Marking irregularities

Marks, instituted for the protection of the craft and the honest men within it, are of great importance, but they

APPRECIATING SILVER

are no foolproof guide to date unless other points are taken into consideration. An understanding of style, in any country at any date, comes first, for while some pieces of every age and quality are incorrectly marked, others, quite legitimately, bear no marks at all, even within a strictly controlled system like that of England. Quantities of high-class silver in the 16th and 17th centuries, made to commission and therefore not for sale, were marked only by the maker; much early provincial silver bore unofficial marks or none at all, because of distance from an assay office, while all small objects weighing less than $\frac{1}{4}$ oz troy, or highly decorated pieces were exempt, in their case because punches, larger than those used on the continent, might cause damage. Every country had its own particular problems leading to diverse irregularities, but these mentioned are typical of the sort of reasoning behind them.

Armorials

Armorials provide another clue towards dating silver, particularly in the style of the decorative cartouche surrounding the shield. This cartouche tends to be more imposing on British work, but there is much in this very large subject that is common to all, including the importance of *contemporary* application, for a later date, particularly when preceded by erasure, detracts from value. In England, where armorials were usually engraved, they were used so invariably from about 1660–1830 that anything lacking them invites suspicion; their use on the continent was less constant, and they were more frequently cast and applied, embossed or stamped.

These armorials derive from the motifs (charges) that were painted on a warrior's shield as his personal symbol and depend on color for certain identification for, although a crest may be common to several families, no two coats of arms in full color are identical, although they may appear to be so in black and white. A scheme was therefore devised in Italy in the early 17th century for indicating tinctures (colors) by hatchment (shading) on the shield and although this was rarely seen before about 1700 its use has been fairly constant ever since and is best described by illustration.

The shield may be impaled (halved, or parted), which usually, though not invariably, indicates a marriage; such arms show the husband's charges on the dexter side which, while appearing to be on the left was actually on the right side to the warrior whose hand is behind it; the arms in the sinister side are those of the wife's father. When a small shield is super-imposed centrally over another it is described as "in pretence" and signifies that the wife is an heiress. Parting is found on the continent, but two shields side by side (*acollé*) are more usual and were also used occasionally in England. Quartering is another method of assembling arms of two or more interests on the same shield, the charges of two families, for instance, appearing top and bottom of opposite sides, while multiple interests take a quarter each.

A full achievement of armorial bearings is rarely emblazoned on silver, yet its composition should be understood, for any permutation of its factors may be used at any time, in any place, in addition to the constant shield. The crest, important because it is used alone, or with a coronet on small wares, appears at the top above a helm (the warrior's helmet) with the coronet of nobility or a twist of colored silk, signifying the cap of estate, below it, immediately above the shield. The cartouche surrounds the shield, spreading out above it in Holland, but mainly to the sides in England, where its use on silver is more constant, diminishing in importance when supporters are used,

Hatchments depicting colors on armorial shields. *L to R:* Azure (blue), Gules (red), Vert (green), Sable (black), *bottom row:* Purpure (purple), Or (gold), Argent (silver), Ermine.

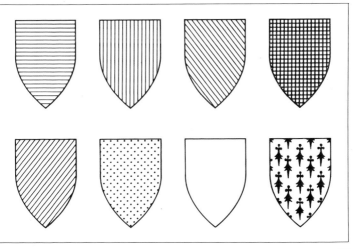

APPRECIATING SILVER

for it is a decorative addition, at the option of the maker, not an intrinsic part of the bearings. Supporters, usually heraldic beasts, were added originally for their splendid effect and tend to be more important in France, where they stand further apart from the shield than in England. They are not necessarily an indication of nobility, for anyone could use them originally and change them at will. A motto also appears below the shield in England, but *above* it in Scotland.

The styles of the cartouches mostly originated in France and where used on silver are a valuable clue to date when applied contemporaneously, although certain overlapping must be allowed for, in addition to provincial time lagging. Feather mantling is the first recognized form, feathering out from one side only of a central rib to start with, later from both, and although dates vary slightly according to national usage of style, this was in vogue roughly from 1660–85. Scrolling foliage (*c* 1675–1700) developed from it, growing in elaboration until it became baroque (*c* 1700–1735), when any spaces in the scrolling foliage were filled in with brickwork, escallop shells or masks appearing above and below the shield; animals also appear on some of the later examples, but *within* the cartouche and not to be confused with supporters, which are outside it.

The greatest difference between this and the next phase (*c*1735–70), is the asymmetric rococo shape and flowing style, for the more exuberant motifs of rococo are not used, scrolls, in particular, flowers and foliage generally sufficing. Exceptions to the rule of engraved armorials in England mainly appear at this time, for on richly decorated pieces they too are cast and applied or embossed. Symmetry returned with neo-classicism (*c*1780–1800), ribbons, husks, and other flowing motifs being mainly responsible for the light effect, enhanced by an attractive draped mantling on larger pieces. Engraving was once more the rule in England and when bright-cut is keenly sought by collectors. No cartouche was used between about 1800–1805, after which a virtual repetition of the scrolling foliage of the late 17th century was executed with mechanical precision and little charm.

The coronet is an invaluable guide to rank and where changes in status have taken place, is also a help in dating unmarked silver (for instance, a viscount's coronet above the armorials of a family elevated to a

FLUCTUATING PRICES

dukedom at a known date, narrows possibility considerably). The formation of these coronets is international and precisely defined: that of a duke is surmounted by strawberry leaves, a marquess by strawberry leaves punctuated by balls, an earl by balls lifted high on projecting points with a trefoil at the lower level between them; a viscount has adjoining small balls and a baron larger balls, well spread out.

Fluctuating prices

Armorials in their original state are a mark of quality, but price is not necessarily connected with value and when quality is absent may prove extremely fickle. Examples of this arise when the popularity of a maker causes his work to command immensely more than that of contemporary craftsmen producing silver of equal or even better standard, when an object bears very rare hallmarks (avidly bid for by collectors who specialise in the subject) or when one individual sets out to buy up a subject, regardless of cost, and then stops, causing disaster to the speculator as prices tumble. At the time of writing the prices of early spoons and sets of flatware are rising rapidly, while those of sauce ladles (c 1800) are beginning to fall. Tomorrow the pattern may change, for only quality is constant.

A fine pierced basket by Peter Archambo, London, 1736, with chased handle and scroll and shell border, with clearly engraved armorials in the center.

APPRECIATING SILVER

Collecting silver

What to collect is a personal matter, dependent on space and cash available and temperament. Taste, personal interests and availability dictate the frequency of buying and govern the pleasure a subject may hold years later. To be enjoyed, silver must be appreciated and this entails careful selection, searching for weak points where damage may soon occur if it has not already, such as the bow end of sugar tongs, a domed cover where silver has been hammered up and may be thin causing pinprick holes to appear, joints where handles, spouts or feet may have received rough treatment, pushing them into the body, or the rims of simple sauceboats or cups unprotected by strengthening decoration.

Caring for silver

Finally, there is the matter of care, for both patina and marks may be damaged by abrasive cleaning, while many of the processes used to restore badly neglected silver by small-time professionals, such as buffing with pumice, are suitable only in the final stages of manufacture, and even then are not used after planishing. Some commercial silver polishes also remove the glow from old silver but, because it is convenient, a stary, over-white surface may sometimes be seen on silver displayed by retailers. Constant, careful handling is the best method of maintaining silver, washing by hand in warm soapy water (or a mild detergent) and rubbing dry with a soft cloth. Depressions in chased silver require a brush and ammonia which, followed by chalk, will help to clean the awkward places. Some commercial cleaners are excellent, but a warm water rinse and careful drying should follow their use. The higher the standard of silver the warmer the patination, but such soft silver scratches more easily. The pure silver used for electroplating both tarnishes and scratches the most of all, and in its failure to respond to loving care, will cause inevitable disappointment.

GUIDE TO
SILVER

Ewer made to
accompany the dish
on p. 23. Genoa,
1619.

EARLY EUROPEAN SILVER

A very brief résumé outlining the style and purpose of some of Europe's finest silver, reflecting the lavish periods in the history of the countries concerned and now mostly in museums.

HORNS

Horns were man's natural drinking vessels. Mounted in richly decorated silver for the wealthy, so preserving them, horns are also steeped in historical and legal interest. (Nautilus shells, coconuts, ostrich shells etc, were also used according to locality).

MAZERS

The finest of these very early wooden drinking bowls, preserved by mounting with a silver lip and base, also had a raised boss inside (an applied plaque), that could be truly magnificently decorated. Standing mazers, raised on a stem, were most beautifully made in 16th-century Scotland.

TAZZE

A 16th-century shallow standing dish originating in Italy and made widely, varying according to national

Below L: Silver gilt horn, German, *c* 1450.

Bottom L: English mazer, 1501. Only the bowls of the rich were silver mounted and have therefore survived.

EARLY EUROPEAN SILVER

tastes. Usually a boss (or in Germany a statuesque figure) inside the bowl. Dessert stands or standing salvers are frequently misnamed "Tazze." A shallow dish on a short stem, derived from Valencia pottery was special to Spain and Portugal in the 15th and 16th centuries.

STANDING CUPS

Amongst the most varied of ceremonial plate, these tall cups were raised on a stem and completed by a high cover. Decoration, according to region and date, was usually on the grand scale and *might* include coconuts, glass or other materials. After *c* 1660 two-handled cups were made for ceremonial use.

DOUBLE CUP

16th-century German palindromic speciality, in a standing cup or mazer form.

ANIMAL CUP

16th-century German Guild cup, formed as models of animals or birds.

GOURD CUPS

Standing cups with a gourd-shaped bowl and a tall stem. German (*c* 1570–1620) and English (when possibly German made), sometimes with a steeple.

GLOBE CUP

Standing cup (*c* 1580–1610) a strongly modeled

Below: Two standing cups from Nuremburg, one 1600, and the pineapple 1650.

Below R: The Galloway Mazer, by James Gray of Canongate, 1569. The standing mazer was a Scottish speciality.

EARLY EUROPEAN SILVER

figure supporting an engraved globe; popular in Germany and Switzerland.

FONT CUP
Flat based, font-shaped English standing cup, c 1500–75.

STEEPLE CUPS
Standing cups made only in England, c 1590–1640, and distinguishable by an egg-shaped bowl on a trumpet foot, surmounted by a pierced steeple.

EWERS AND BASINS
These were of paramount importance to medieval dining when hands required continual rinsing with rosewater. Made to the highest standards in almost all countries, but especially in Antwerp, Portugal and Spain, where they were particularly popular.

GREAT SALT
This was placed before the host on the medieval table in England, with the principal guests nearby, with smaller salts further down the table. Elaborately

English steeple cup.

The Vyvyan Salt, London, 1592; silver gilt inset with painted glass.

EARLY EUROPEAN SILVER

architectural in form, those of hour-glass shape were peculiar to England, as were the bell salts (1580–1620). (See also *The Dinner Table*.)

NEF

A status symbol formed as a ship, placed on the table before the host in medieval France, where most commonly made. Small examples served as salts. Model ships on wheels were also made ornamentally in Germany.

FURNITURE

Beds, chairs, tables, mirrors and fireside accessories made in solid silver or coated in silver leaf, were made in the more extravagant courts of Europe, such as that of Louis XIV at Versailles, in the 16th and 17th centuries.

TIGERWARE JUGS

Imported from the Rhine, and silver-mounted in England, 16th century, when Chinese porcelain, serpentine and other ewers, tankards, bowls and jugs were similarly treated.

The Burghley Nef, by Pierre Le Flamand, Paris, 1482. Silver gilt, of incredibly detailed workmanship mounted on a Nautilus shell.

CHURCH PLATE

From the official adoption of Christianity as the religion of the Roman Empire until the height of the middle ages the creation of articles for use in or adornment of the church was the goldsmith's prime occupation. Fine pieces of gold and silver were made to the glory of God, often set with precious stones and usually incorporating the sacred monogram IHS, the first three letters of Jesus, when written in Greek, which may also be taken as representing the Latin "In Hoc Signo Vinces" In this sign *(the cross)* shall you conquer.

From the first everything required for the Mass was made, with different forms being introduced for Protestant worship.

CHALICE
The cup in which wine is consecrated at Mass and the most important object directly concerned with the life of any Catholic church. Standards varied according to the wealth of each parish, the finest being quite magnificent, inset with lovely enamels and rich jewelry. The dating of a chalice made between 1200 and 1540 is ascertainable by style to within fifty years and, despite the deprivations of the reformation, more such chalices survive than any other early objects, except for spoons.

COMMUNION CUPS
Cups with a larger bowl than the massing chalices which they replaced in the Anglican (Episcopalian) Church, by order of Edward VI. They were basically of beaker shape on a stem with a foot, a plain reversible cover also acting as a paten, as it always had. Although frequently described as a chalice the English Elizabethan communion cup is distinctly different and always identifiable as such. Any on which a sacred symbol is found, if not pre-Reformation, date from the early 17th century when Archbishop Laud tried to restore some of the old ritual. Such cups, made in the chalice fom extant 1525–40 are rare.

BEAKERS
Large dual-purpose vessels in which the wine could be passed among the congregation in the reformed church of countries such as Germany, Scotland, America and Scandinavia.

FLAGON
Vessel in which wine could be brought to the altar in England to replenish the communion cup. A few 16th-

English communion cup, 1570, with paten cover. These were always distinctively more simple than the massing chalice.

Spanish parcel gilt chalice c 1670, with epoussé and chased decoration.

One of a pair of parcel gilt livery pots or flagons, English, 1590.

CHURCH PLATE

century pot-bellied Livery pots or flagons (a word adopted only after 1640) were made, but the vast majority date from 1630, when their use became compulsory. These are in tall cylindrical tankard form, with a good lid and handle, and are usually engraved with an inscription and occasionally the arms of the donor, although magnificent examples exist decorated overall.

CRUET

The vessels — two small bottles — brought to the altar, from which wine and water were mixed in the chalice in the Mass.

CIBORIUM

A broad, shallow bowl with a tightly fitting cover, in the form of a chalice, in which the Host, the bread or wafer of the Mass, is taken to the congregation.

MONSTRANCE

A transparent vessel (from c 14th century) in which the Host was displayed behind rock crystal, magnificently mounted in the manner of a standing cup in medieval times.

PYX

A small, round box, used from the 6th century for the reservation of a portion of the consecrated Host, ready for immediate use by the sick, to whom it could be carried. Often richly decorated, with a conical lid from which it could be suspended above the altar. Later it had a flat lid and developed into a standing pyx (c 1500) soon becoming indistinguishable from a monstrance. In England the pyx was often contained in the ciborium, itself hung above the altar, but it ceased to be used at the Reformation, except for recusant examples.

PATEN

The plate on which the communion bread or wafer is served.

CHRISMATORY

A small casket, sometimes of trefoil shape in which were kept the three holy oils used since the 3rd century for the sick, those to be confirmed and in baptism.

COMMUNION SET

Miniature set which replaced the Chrismatory and pyx (from 1684) in England.

BAPTISMAL BASIN

The Font was sometimes supplemented by a font basin near the altar, and in Scotland and New England in particular a baptismal basin replaces the font. An alms dish (on which the collection was taken to the altar for

Hanging censer, English, mid 14th century.

Head of a medieval crozier in gothic style.

Italian reliquary c 1600, in which relics are kept in little compartments within the cross and not in the crystal skull as might be expected.

blessing) was often used and rosewater dishes were sometimes bequeathed for the purpose.

CROSS

Processional crosses (originating in the 6th century) are decorated on both sides. The altar cross, placed between candlesticks from the time the altar was sited against the eastern wall of a church about the 12th century, is decorated on one side only and usually depicts Christ crucified. When either form was revived in protestant churches it was usually without the figure of Christ.

PECTORAL CROSS

Could apply to any cross worn around the neck but understood to mean that worn by a bishop which, during the middle ages, contained a fragment of the True Cross.

CROZIER

The pastoral staff of a bishop or abbot, received at his consecration. The heads of Celtic and medieval croziers were among the most splendid of all objects made for the church, more of which survive in constantly Roman Catholic countries, including Canada, than in those affected by the reformation.

CHURCH PLATE

ALTAR CANDLESTICKS
Generally large, up to 940 mm (37 in) high, they were used in pairs in England, sixes more generally on the Continent. When in silver truly magnificent, richly decorated in baroque form, set on a tripod base and, up to *c* 1660 fitted with a pricket holder in place of the more familiar socket.

SANCTUS BELL
Rung during the Mass itself and to warn people of the presence of the Sacrament when carried in the pyx.

RELIQUARY
A casket or other housing for the bones of saints and other holy relics. Of great spiritual importance, they attracted the finest workmanship and ornament and may be small containers in which relics could be carried on the person or those used to display such relics on an altar, which often take the form of a representation of the part of the body contained within. A shrine is a large reliquary.

CENSER (THURIBLE)
A swinging vessel in which incense is laid on burning charcoal, developed *c* 9th century, consists of a metal bowl with three chains attached and a removable perforated cover which could be architectural but took many magnificent forms.

INCENSE BOAT
A container in which incense is carried to the altar, it sometimes has a spoon attached.

A fine example of a Dutch monstrance, Haarlem, 1674.

Two Spanish pyx boxes, dated 1620.

THE SERVICE OF WINE

The word "wine" here is generic, for this section covers all objects used for the preparation and service of convivial drinks.

WINE COOLERS

Vessels for holding a single bottle of wine in cold water or ice, fitted with a detachable liner and frequently made in sets of two or four. Although uncommon before 1780, English examples derived from classical pottery survive from *c* 1700, they are mostly in varied vase shapes with small ring or loop handles, which later were occasionally fantastic. A staved bucket form was also popular and many copies or designs based on the Warwick vase appear from 1812, the best by Paul Storr. They were prolifically made in all forms in Sheffield plate. Coolers are very rare in America but continental wine growing countries made them from the 17th century, particularly France in the sumptuous Versailles period of Louis XIV. The word 'Sechielli," which describes such vessels in Italy, is also applied to attractive engraved or embossed bulbous jars with a narrow neck, used there for carrying liquids.

Ice buckets developed from the cooler, copying the bucket form exactly, and with their wide mouths were considerably more practical.

WINE CISTERNS

Oval basins for the cooling of many bottles at a banquet from *c* 1660–1870, with a flat everted rim, four lion's paw or dolphin feet in the late 17th century, or a wide rim-foot after about 1700, and handles based on a family's armorial supporters or rings suspended from a lion's mask. The few continental examples are similar in concept, survivors largely belong to England's great families who looked on size as a status symbol, rising from one of 28350 g (1,000 oz) that Charles II had made for his French mistress, to one of 85050 g (3,000 oz, the size of a modern bath tub) by Charles Kandler, 1734, now in Leningrad.

WINE FOUNTAINS

Large (50–100cm/20–40in high), urn-shaped vessels with a spigot for the easy serving of decanted wine at a banquet, often made *en suite* with a cistern. Magnificent sculptural and architectural continental fountains are known from the early 16th century (particularly from France and Germany) but, although earlier examples were recorded, the main period in England was *c* 1680–1740. Smaller 18th-century urns

A pair of staved ice buckets by Paul Storr, London, 1830, the foremost maker of the staved ice cooler.

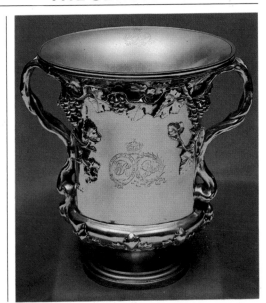

Bell-shaped wine cooler by William Bellchamber, London, 1835 with embossed vine decoration.

THE SERVICE OF WINE

intended for tea or coffee were mostly fitted with a means of retaining heat. Those lacking such a device may have been intended for cold drinks.

JUGS

There are many types of jug but almost none has been used exclusively for its original purpose, which by now is often obscure. When forks became popular (c 1650) ewers that had been necessary for finger rinsing at table were often used as serving jugs, those with a cover being well suited to mulled wine; ewers made from 1660, including those of lovely helmet shape with harp handles introduced into many countries by the Huguenots, *may* have been made for the purpose but were more often part of a toilet set, or intended for sideboard decoration. Covered jugs die out about 1725 except for those intended for coffee, chocolate or milk, while those with a wooden or wickerwork handle (or that could once have been wickered) were also intended for hot fluids. Beer jugs tend to be somewhat more squat and American jugs for iced water to be very large, but all countries made jugs for their preferred drinks, keeping fairly simple within the styles of each period according to national interpretation, with occasional variations: for instance, the English sometimes copied pottery shapes in the early 18th century, while the Americans alone copied Liverpool cream-ware porcelain, c 1800. In England pear-shaped jugs were made from about 1730, often large; ornate

Covered jug by Richard Raine, London, 1712, in very heavy quality silver, with a French wine taster, by Joseph le Boeuf, Lorient, c 1740.

THE SERVICE OF WINE

rococo was largely confined to those intended for sideboard decoration; the formal Adam style of neoclassicism arrived c1760, soon giving way to tall, simple elegance. Glass claret jugs with silver mounts, or a silver design overlaid on glass date from c1820, Australia also making these from 1850.

WINE TASTERS

Vessels used during the Middle Ages for professional tasters to test wine for poison, but more often for the vintner or buyer to sample wines. In England and Portugal these are small shallow bowls with a high central dome against which the color of the wine is clearly seen. Elsewhere, with the majority of survivors coming from France (18th and early 19th centuries), these small bowls (about 75 mm/3 in diam) have a single snake handle, a pierced lug with a ring beneath it, or a kidney-shaped thumbpiece, often with a name engraved under the rim. During the late 17th century sweetmeat dishes, frequently described as wine

A German wine fountain, c 18th century showing typical Nuremburg pineapple lobing and rococo decoration.

THE SERVICE OF WINE

tasters, were made in thin silver in England and Germany with punched decoration and twisted rope or shell handles, and could have been used as such, or for a variety of purposes, whatever the original intention. A dram cup, *c* 1651 by Hull and Sanderson of Boston, possibly the oldest piece of surviving American silver, is virtually identical.

PIPKIN (or Brandy Warmer)
A small saucepan with straight wooden handle.

WINE COASTERS
Circular stands for one bottle or decanter, with pierced or solid silver sides of varied form, usually with a wooden, baize-covered base. Made from 1760, often in pairs or multiples of them, mostly in England where port drinking after dinner, without servants present, was traditional for gentlemen. Double coasters, offering a choice of bottle, were made from 1795, often in jolly boat form, or as wagons from 1820. Made prolifically in Sheffield plate from 1790 in every form known in silver.

PILGRIM BOTTLES
Originated from the flasks carried by pilgrims and were made from about 1550–1715 (with 19th-century reproductions). Too large for carrying, these flattened

A heavy wine coaster in undecorated form by William Allen, London, 1800, and a fine lobed coaster with turn-over rim by William Burwash and Richard Dibley, London, 1809.

Below: A pair of pierced wine coasters by Hester Bateman, with beaded rims, London, 1783.

THE SERVICE OF WINE

pear-shaped bottles with pendant chain handles hanging from their stoppers were mostly intended as sideboard pieces and may be found in some of England's great homes; similar German bottles are less decorative and scent flasks may appear in similar form on a smaller scale.

WINE FUNNELS

Used for straining wine into a decanter or bottle from about 1660, becoming popular *c* 1770. Usually plain or with a simple border, some are fitted with a strainer; others have a ribbed stem to allow air bubbles to escape, or a curved tip, to prevent air from entering the bottle.

PUNCH BOWLS AND MONTEITHS

The five ingredients of punch, which derived from India, were mixed formally at table in a large, round bowl, averaging about 250 mm (10 in) across. Surviving punch bowls date from *c* 1680 and monteiths, which have a notched rim, from 1683. One explanation for this rim is that glasses were brought to table suspended in iced water by their feet, but as punch is a hot drink it is more logical to assume that glasses were simply transported this way in the empty bowl. Early monteiths were comparatively simple, with fluted

Pair of lobed wine coasters by Emes and Barnard, Sheffield 1817, and two embossed coasters by Smith, Tate Hoult and Tate, 1822 and by T. Blagdon & Co, 1826, both of Sheffield.

Below: Two wine coasters from a set of six by Robert Hennell, London, 1774, with applied neo-classic motifs.

THE SERVICE OF WINE

panels below the notches, decorated only with engraved armorials or chinoiseries, but by 1690, when the notched rim first became detachable, decoration was heavier, with overall flutes, decorated straps, gadroons, shells and masks. These detachable borders, which rendered the two types of bowl interchangeable, have often now been lost but differentiation is not difficult for the upper edge of monteiths, the majority of all such bowls, was more rigid, while from c 1700–1730 they usually had lion's-mask drop-ring handles, the punch bowl (which might also have a cover), had them only sometimes. Either type was set on a low rim foot, becoming higher with time, very noticeably so by 1715. Irish punch bowls were rare (and monteiths more so), smaller than in England but of fine quality and usually set on three feet, in the manner of their smaller rococo bowls. At least one American punch bowl, by John Burt (1692–1745), was also set on three hoof feet. Several large, multi-purposed cups with two cast scroll handles on a flat rim base were made in America and called punch bowls, following the lead of Jeremiah Dummer in 1692, but the plain round bowl on a low base is more usual in the 18th century, deep, as with Paul Revere's famous

A late form of punch bowl made by Hester Bateman, London, 1784, made for Chester Corporation.

"Sons of Liberty" bowl, but more often comparatively shallow and elegant. Monteiths were rare and (except for copies) made before 1700, while in England popularity waned only after 1730, the punch bowl surviving until about 1775. Smaller bowls of any type undoubtedly were used for punch in the home, one of the most attractive being the Dutch-inspired early New York six-paneled shallow bowl, 150–330 mm (6–13 in) across. Continental punch bowls were distinctly national; shallow, notched and without a cover in France (late 18th century), probably intended for cooling glasses, while the Scandinavians made a shallow bowl which, in the mid-17th century, was very similar to the Dutch New York bowl, with caryatid scroll handles, becoming more like a French écuelle in body by 1680 but set on three ball feet (decorated in Sweden) and with swan neck scroll handles, terminating in a similar ball.

PUNCH LADLES

Used for the service of punch. Of plain round form before 1700, with a wooden or tubular silver handle set at an angle of 45°; shaped or fancy bowls arrived c 1740. By 1760 they had lost importance and were of thinner silver, with a twisted whalebone handle.

A very rare form of punch bowl by John Elston of Exeter, 1708. The detachable montieth rim is very usual, but the spigot tap is very rare indeed as is the lack of handles before c 1730.

THE SERVICE OF WINE

TODDY LADLES

Very small silver-bowled 19th century ladles, with steeply set whalebone handles; Scottish made and intended for the service of strong toddy, which is hot spiced liquor.

STRAINER

Made from early times for many purposes (straining rough wine, spices for mulled wine etc). Those intended for punch were wide enough to fit over the bowl, had two superbly cut or cast lug handles (sometimes of shaped wire) and very fine piercing in the bowl. They date from 1750 in England and America (Scotland 1800). Irish strainers were similar from 1750, but were also made from c1720 pierced with regular holes, two simply-pierced flat lugs and of great breadth. Those for tea, for instance, would fit over a teacup. Rather earlier, c1730, are rare circular bowls, probably intended for punch, pierced centrally, with a single ring handle and a clip to attach to the punch bowl.

NUTMEG GRATERS

Also used in making punch (see *Small Collectables*).

An early spice box with scallop shell lid and feet, 1617.

Below: A strainer with wide handles for use with a punch bowl, by Edward Aldridge, London, 1768.

THE SERVICE OF WINE

Kovsh.

KOVSH

A Byzantine-style, boat-shaped drinking vessel or ladle with one handle, made exclusively in Russia, originally for drinking or serving drinks such as Kvass; about 9 in long. They became more ornate in the 18th century when presented as a symbol of honor. Numerous 19th-century reproductions of 17th-century styles exist.

WINE LABELS

Used for identifying unlabelled bottles or decanters (see *Small Collectables*).

SPICE BOXES

Spices were used in making punch or for mulling wine and boxes for them were introduced mid 16th century; escallop shell covers (pre *c* 1625) were set on four shell feet and were divided inside. Oval spice or sugar boxes were made from about 1660 (use interchangeable), but the oval or oblong box (*c* 1695–1725) with a hinged double lid on four feet often incorporated a nutmeg grater, fixing purpose. This type originated in France where it was very small (50–63mm/2–2½in), often gadrooned and beautifully engraved or flat chased. Casters (see *The Dining Table*) took their place.

Double-lidded spice box by Frederick Kandler, London, 1735.

Below: Sugar or sweetmeat box, 1676, in lobed design with coiled handle and conch shell feet.

THE SERVICE OF WINE

SUGAR BOXES

Shallow caskets which may also have been used for other purposes, first seen in the 17th century when English examples were oval, with strongly curved sides, often lobed and sometimes gadrooned, set on four feet and with an entwined serpent or otherwise scrolled handle on the lid. Popular in America with Boston's earliest makers, who copied the English type to magnificent effect from *c* 1700 but which were soon replaced by casters. Continental 18th-century examples (mostly German) are similar in shape, decorated in national period styles, and sometimes higher, like a bowl which was made concurrently.

Fine quality covered sugar bowl by John Swift, London, 1734.

Sugar box, 1650 by one of London's finest unidentified makers, using a hound sejant as mark.

DRINKING VESSELS

Of interest to all people, for every nation has had its drinking vessels since time began.

TANKARDS

Cylindrical vessels with a hinged lid, thumb-piece and handle. Mainly used for beer and made in most northern countries, from the early 16th century.

Before 1700. From the start tankards showed regional variations, those in Germany having small tapering bodies, soon becoming large and very ornate, embossed overall to tell a biblical or mythological story and with an intricately cast handle. In Scandinavia (Norway and Denmark were united until 1814), they were tall and thin, although considerably less so than a flagon, with slightly tapering sides, concave base and stepped, rounded lid, sometimes with a coin inserted. The base and lid may be chased, the body lightly engraved, usually with fruit or flowers, while a band of molding, such as ropework, was usual near the base. Towards the end of the 16th century comparative breadth gradually increased.

The earliest tankards in England were pear-shaped with a rounded lid and molded foot, lightly engraved with arabesques, but by the 1560s they had become

R : Silver gilt German tankard, *c* 1600 embossed overall.

Below L : Swedish Peg tankard, Stockholm, late 17th century with handle and broad, squat shape characteristically embossed.

DRINKING VESSELS

very similar to the early Scandinavian type. This style broadened slightly and became less tall during the first half of the 17th century, when plain cylindrical tankards were made, with no base, but a flat cover, protruding in front, and a solid thumbpiece like a breaking wave. During the Commonwealth the distinctive feature was the skirted base, usually with an otherwise plain matted body, and while early-17th-century silver is rare in England because of the Civil War, a few pieces survive, including some examples of silver-mounted serpentine.

In Germany vast parcel gilt cylindrical tankards on a molded foot continued to be narrative, or were chased overall with scrolling strapwork, human masks, flowers or other motifs on a matted ground, sometimes partially pierced, with a solid "sleeve" inside. In Danzig the same might be varied by coins from any one given state, inserted overall. In Hungary tankards were tall and distinctly shaped, narrowing in mid body and sometimes hexagonal or octagonal, with or without medallions of Roman masks.

The distinctive Scandinavian peg tankard was introduced in about 1650 and is notable for the row of eight pegs evenly spaced inside behind the handle,

Below: The German tankard of 1620 has become less tapered and tall, but is still embossed, those of the north remaining tall, as *R*, 1630.

R: Peg tankard by John Plummer, York, 1663, with his distinctive flower engraving, open to show pegs, and *far R*, closed.

Below R: Squat silver gilt and niello tankard In the Russian style, late 17th century, and *R*, a Danish Tankard by Jonan Andersen, Elsinore, 1686.

DRINKING VESSELS

designed to ensure fair shares in communal drinking. These large, or very large tankards have a broad, squat drum-shaped body, with a rounded cover and base, set on three feet of ball and claw, pomegranate, or sometimes lion couchant form. The thumbpiece usually matches the feet, but may vary within the range. The body is generally plain, the lid engraved, usually with fruit or flowers. Towards the end of the century chasing is increasingly used, particularly around the foot joins on applied leaf-shaped plaques, with the whole body chased on tankards made in Oslo, or occasionally on those from Bergen. Such tankards continued with only slight changes of degree, for the next two hundred years.

Swedish peg tankards are distinctly more squat, height almost matching width. The feet and thumb-piece are larger and usually pomegranate or ball, heavily embossed. this decoration continuing on over the applied shaped plaque above it. The broad scroll handle is embossed, generally with fruit or flowers, while the plain body tapers slightly towards the base. The low cover protrudes over the top rim and is generally engraved, while those from Norway round off the drum. Similar tankards from the Baltic countries and Russia are also very squat, extensive chasing of stylized flowers, foliage and other motifs becoming increasingly complicated as the century progressed.

Peg tankards of Scandinavian derivation were also made in the north of England and Scotland, chiefly by John Plummer of York, some of them exquisitely engraved with flowers on the body at a time when engraving was usually used exclusively for armorials. The handles of these were never engraved as in Norway, nor chased as in Sweden, although cut card decoration might be found on handle or lid towards the end of the century, particularly in Scotland. Pomegranate feet, their jointure strengthened by applied leaf scrolls, the thumbpiece not always matching, were the most frequently used. Tankards with feet were not necessarily fitted with pegs and some that are plain inside have a lion thumbpiece, with lion feet if of top quality (sometimes added later to less important silver). The normal tankard of the period has a slightly tapered drum-shaped body, set on a flat molded base: a stepped flat top and a wide variety of thumbpieces. The body was usually plain, engraved with armorials, but acanthus leaf decoration was occasionally chased

Thumbpieces:

Lion couchant

Openwork

Lion sejant or mask

Cherub

Double-cusp

The Fawdery
tankard, London,
1705, and a German
tankard, 1690, by
Pickjel.

around the lower half, while gadrooning on the rim and slightly protruding base came in about 1690, when cut card applications might also be found on handles or lids. The attractive overall chinoiserie flat chasing was used only during the 1680s. A Newcastle speciality is a long tapering rat tail running down the body under the handle.

In the last quarter of the 17th century tankards of similar shape, but with immense regional variation, were made in America. To start with those from Boston, where they were used in both home and church, were comparatively plain, the stepped lid protruding over the tapered drum, finished with a simple molding at the base, a rat tail running down under the handle, similar to, but shorter than that of Newcastle. This was soon discontinued and from about 1690 cut card applications might be used; deep grooves ran down some handles while gadrooning was also occasionally

DRINKING VESSELS

applied to the steps of the lid. Thumbpieces became more elaborate and a good cast mask was frequently applied to the shaped termination of the handle. Since this was important family silver, initials were almost invariably engraved on the handle and armorial bearings within superb cartouches filled one side of an otherwise plain body. Some New England tankards with coins inserted in their lids showed a degree of Dutch influence there. Armorials were also engraved upon the distinctive New York tankards, magnificently executed in the 17th-century Dutch manner, with tight swirls in bold strokes, swags of fruit under the shield frequently appearing. The main features of these tankards, made from the last decade of the century, were good size with a broad drum; a lid almost domed to a flat top, with a wide, serrated flange, sometimes engraved; usually a corkscrew thumbpiece, with a cast mask or other ornament on the disc-shaped plaque terminating the broad scroll handle, on which a cast lion has frequently been applied, another New York speciality. The molded baseband, its depth giving importance, is characteristically interrupted by a meander wire, and surmounted by a strip of stamped, foliate ornament. Every feature was not always used, and although some provincial New England goldsmiths combined the forms of Boston and New York the New York tankard is unmistakable. From about 1700 the handle might also be applied with cast ornament in the Swedish manner.

After 1700. From the beginning of the 18th century the tankard in England narrowed in proportion to height; the lid gradually raised in a dome, gadrooned at first, surmounted on the largest from London or Edinburgh by a baluster finial, or a crest finial on the grander examples. A molded band soon appeared around the lower part of the body, which became baluster-shaped in about 1730. Variations thereafter were only slight and tankards gradually losing their size and importance, ceased to evolve after about 1790. Because of the 19th-century delight in embossing plain surfaces it is important to note that only acanthus leaves or flutes were ever embossed on English tankards before 1810, except for the short-lived chinoiserie flat chasing.

In Scotland, where claret was long preferred to beer, tankards were only rarely made before 1700 and then were few, large and of superlative quality, particularly

DRINKING VESSELS

Tankard by Augustine Float of Newcastle, c 1690, showing the long rat tail peculiar to the Newcastle area.

Scottish tankard by James Sympson, Edinburgh, 1702.

New York tankard c 1730, with coin inset in lid.

DRINKING VESSELS

when made in Edinburgh. Irish tankards are extremely rare. In America the first Philadelphian tankards to survive date from about 1725, and are of top quality, heavy and broad, with a mid band, the tapered drum curving to a tucked-in base on a substantially molded splayed foot. The cover is domed, without the finial used in Boston, where the body is taller, slimmer, and slightly more tapered towards the dome, its cover flange turning down characteristically. The cast mask on the handle end, now in disc form, is still frequently used, but became rare during the second half of the century, when the flame finial was the only other change. At this same period Philadelphian tankards became slimmer and taller with a higher dome and higher splayed foot. Usually baluster, straight sides did

also occur. The openwork thumbpiece was typical and so was the manner in which double scroll handles joined, like two hands in prayer. New York basically retained its old form, but without the stamped ornament above or the meander wire within the baseband, itself flatter to the body than those of Philadelphia or Boston. The lid remained a flat-topped dome, usually with a coin inserted, and the flange was no longer engraved, although applied ornament of fruit, flowers or geometric design enriched the broad handle, still terminating in a good mask. This remained the basic shape, without most of the early embellishments, a fine double scroll handle, characteristically differing from those of Philadelphia. Midbands, although not unheard of, were seldom used.

Two Queen Anne mugs, by Timbrell and Bentley 1713 and Nathaniel Locke, 1716, in plain form; both London. See p. 92.

THE GUIDE

MUGS

Mainly made in England (surviving from 1660), or as CANNS in America about 1695, but only occasionally on the continent. A cylindrical drinking vessel *without a lid*, generally following the form of contemporary tankards in $\frac{1}{2}$ pint or pint size, with cast S scroll handles. A very attractive bulbous mug is an exception to this generalization, which has a narrow, comparatively tall, reeded cylindrical neck and flat reeded handle, usually decorated in chinoiserie and made in the 1680s. Another style closely resembles a teacup and is encircled by a molded rib at the point where the bottom of the flat, reeded C scroll handle is joined to the body. Below the rib the otherwise clear surface is broken by spiral flutes, giving a slightly bulbous effect. Such mugs were made in England and Scotland. Very rare, but equally attractive, is a transitional mug half way between these two, in style more like an English porringer, with one beaded S scroll handle. The Thistle Cup, peculiar to Scotland, is also shaped like a teacup and was made in Edinburgh from 1680 to 1700, or later in the provinces. The molded rib of this mug rings the body in the upper half, above which the plain surface flares considerably. Set on a flared foot, its rounded base is decorated with a calyx of rising lobes, while its attractive S scroll handle is sometimes enriched with beaded drops. The type of cylindrical mug resembling a tankard of the 1660s was not made until the close of the century and is usually wholly or partially covered in vertical flutes. The baluster form appeared about 1730, later in America, but without the molded mid-band and generally set on a more emphatic splayed foot. These are sometimes decorated with applied vertical lobes around the base. Mugs, never as important as tankards, sometimes bear imposing arms, but are generally made of thinner silver. They have been made continuously to the present day, many in very small size for children, decorated in every style or mixture of styles, very often with excessive embossing, but sometimes delightfully restrained, with snake handles and mere bands of decoration. Embossing was too frequently applied later to an earlier plain surface and spouts were also added to convert mugs to jugs, to their detriment.

SPOUT CUP

A drinking vessel, often of contemporary tankard form, with a long spout curving up from the base, set at right

A pair of beer barrel type mugs by Martin Hall & Co, Sheffield, 1878.

Four mugs, *L to R*, by John Schofield, 1778, Fuller White, 1754, John Wisdorne, 1719 and Hester Bateman 1782; all London.

DRINKING VESSELS

angles to the handle. Said to be for invalid or infant feeding, many examples are too large for the purpose, and the possibility of the spout having been added to another vessel later must be looked for. Made in Britain and America in the 17th century.

FLAGONS

In the 16th century flagons, then known as "Livery Pots" (the word "flagon" was used only from *c* 1640), were bellied with a deep neck, broad scroll handle and rounded lid. They were set on a high foot and derived, like the word "flacon" from the French. Early 17th-century German examples were fantastic, often in grotesque form, but in England they became tall and cylindrical, following tankard styles thereafter, and were usually undecorated, although early examples may be magnificently engraved or flat chased. They sometimes have a lip if for church use. From *c* 1640–65 they have a skirted base. They are rare, except for copies and gothic revivals made after 1760. (*See also Church Silver*).

BEAKERS

Drinking vessels with no stem or handle, originating from the straight part of a horn. The name derives from Scandinavia but they are found in all countries and are among the earliest silver to survive in any quantity. Typical 15th-century examples from Germany (which influenced all the Baltic states, Scandinavia and Russia) were slightly concave, tapering cylinders set on three feet consisting of fine cast figures, animal or human, with covers rising to a figural or architectural finial, often fantastic. A frieze of castellations or architecturally styled flowers, foliage or other motifs surround the base and form a tracery girdle around the cup's center; there is a gallery above its rim and sometimes also below the finial on the cover. Similar 16th-century Scandinavian beakers (mostly from Bergen) may include masks or suspended rings or discs among the girdles, themselves of a more simple form; feet, when used, are most imaginative but there are no covers and overall measurements, which in Germany go up to 300mm (12in), are consequently much reduced (average 100–150mm/4–6in). Late in the period flat chasing may be found near the top but the Scandinavian style changed basically little, despite the girdles becoming mere moldings and the shape more of a V by the end of the 18th century.

The Dutch, who have always used the beaker in

Tall English flagon
with slightly domed
id and skirted base
1688.

Russian schnapps
beakers made in
Kiev, 1899–1908.

DRINKING VESSELS

church and home, influenced England and Scotland, having traded with Norwich from very early times. It is possibly relevant that the oldest beaker in England, itself not necessarily English, bears the arms of the Bishop of Norwich, while the nearby King's Lynn cup, c1350 (one of England's loveliest pieces), has a beautifully enameled bell-shaped bowl, connected to the stem by a bayonet joint so that it may be detached, possibly for separate use as a beaker. By the mid-16th century, when the Dutch Protestants sought asylum from Spanish rule in Norwich, Dutch beakers were of elegant tapering cylindrical line, with a slightly everted lip and slightly spreading foot, usually engraved with flowers, strapwork and arabesques. Such beakers are known in England as the "Norwich" type, their engraving, except when made in Norwich, somewhat coarse and also including scrolled foliage, interlacing strapwork and pendant festoons. Although very few beakers were used in the church in England the standard Elizabethan Communion cup was of beaker shape (on a knopped and footed stem) and was engraved in similar manner. Covered beakers which were of German inspiration, such as the Magdalen cup,

German double beaker, 1610 and a Russian beaker, 1745, in wide flutes with a bulbous base.

1573, were superb rarities at that time in England.

By the early 17th century Holland was also trading with Scotland and exchanging university students between Leyden and Aberdeen. Dutch engraving was rising to its unsurpassed peak and the beakers brought over from Holland for secular use were magnificently engraved. Some of these were later given to the kirk and Scottish-made copies exist from 1608, but those made in Scotland for the kirk (popular in the Aberdeen area) are considerably plainer. Beakers of the Norwich type were also made for the early church in America, founded by Pilgrim Fathers who lived not far from Norwich and then spent years in Leyden. Such beakers were used in church and home but in Boston, where primarily intended for the church, they frequently bore no more than a church inscription or simple decorative engraving, while New York examples, taller and more elegant (c 1680–1700), were often magnificently engraved. From about 1700 a unique, partially fluted, beaker on a low foot was also popular in America, with a band of gadrooning above, a style used for mugs and porringers in England, c 1685–95.

The 17th-century beaker in Germany (where double

Covered beaker, Augsburg, 1695–1705. German beakers were sometimes really sculptural. And a Scandinavian beaker 1764, typically tapered and engraved.

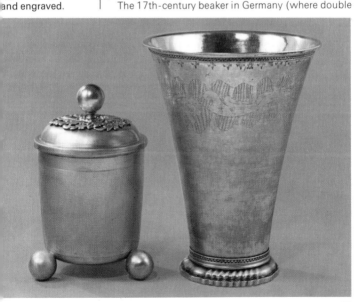

DRINKING VESSELS

beakers in the form of barrels were more prevalent than elsewhere) was mostly set on a molded base, although plain ball feet did still occur, and were usually highly embossed — occasionally flat chased — with mythological, sporting or other scenes, fruit, flowers etc. occasionally also incorporating a matted band. Covers were now rare, but did occur particularly in the Baltic states, which produced very fine beakers, occasionally in gold, of similar form. With the exception of some 18th-century Russian (of rather squat form with niello still favored), Scandinavian and Baltic examples, beakers of the 17th and 18th centuries everywhere were very small, often used as Christening presents, broader in proportion and less elegant. In England beakers of this size were often plain or with a calyx of acanthus leaves around the base, embossed flowers (no scenes) usually reserved for slightly larger examples. Beakers were not featured in Italy and were mostly plain although some filigree-covered examples were made in Genoa, c 1700–1810.

Nests of beakers were also made from early times in many countries, either for church use or for picnicking, particularly on hunting parties. Such sets, which fitted together and had one common cover, were necessarily

Set of six silver gilt beakers by John Bridge, London, 1828.

98

without feet and decorated only around the top, usually with a simple, rib-like molding.

Camp cups, made in the 18th century for military use on campaign, fit in like manner but are rather sturdier.

The majority of surviving French beakers date from the 18th century, although a magnificent gold example (first half 17th century) shows that France always had a style of her own, which was bell-shaped and round-bottomed on a molded low pedestal foot. Within this unchanging basic formula style followed period. The spirally fluted, magnificently engraved gold piece tapered from a straight lip, while swirling rococo waves break over a beaker with a slightly everted rim in 1731, a constant feature thereafter, when matted backgrounds are usual, sometimes with gadroons, a calyx of straps below a mid rib, or a flat chased band of decoration near the top.

JULEP CUP

A straight-sided beaker tapering towards the base from half way; made in America for long, cool drinks, usually in sets, from *c* 1800.

TUMBLER CUP

Made in England *c* 1660 through the 18th century; round cups with straight sides, usually of greater

A tumbler cup by Richard Richardson of Chester, where these cups were always well made, 1742. A stirrup cup in the form of a fox head by Edward Robinson, 1806. See p. 100.

DRINKING VESSELS

breadth than height, characterized by weight in the rounded base which enables them always to right themselves. Sometimes made in sets; used as prizes for racing and cock fighting, or for drinking in a moving carriage. Varying in size from tiny to about 90mm ($3\frac{1}{2}$in), they are usually plain with armorial engraving, but may have acanthus leaf or fluting on the lower half; chinoiserie or embossing rare. The Continental equivalent has a flat, kick-in base.

STIRRUP CUP

A cup without a handle or base, passed to mounted horsemen before hunting, from 1765–1830. Normally formed as a fox's mask, though the head of a greyhound or hare is known. Superseded by a cylindrical saddle flask. Mainly an English speciality but also made in Germany.

WAGER CUP

A festive drinking vessel originating in the Rhine Valley of Germany (late 16th mid 17th century). A double cup of heavy silver, lightly embossed, the larger one formed

Stirrup cup holder by Edward Aldridge, London, 1760.

Wager cup

as a long-skirted woman with a smaller, pivoted cup held in outstretched arms above her head. On bibulous occasions revelers tried to drink from the skirt without spilling from the smaller cup, but, in Holland, where they were known as Bridal Cups, a bridegroom had to drink from the larger and pass the smaller to his bride. These were occasionally copied elsewhere. The Dutch Windmill cup developed from this, becoming very popular up to the 19th century. The skirt, embossed in Dutch style is surmounted by a windmill, to which a tubed ladder leads. When blown, the sails turn (and the reveler starts drinking fast), the dialed number on the back at which they stop indicating the number of cupfuls then to be drunk by any who has failed to empty the skirt in time.

GLASS HOLDERS

A Dutch speciality for holding a drinking glass, mainly made c 1650–90, usually in sets of a dozen, in high relief and statuesque form. Later made elsewhere in similar style.

Dutch windmill cup, c 1620, engraved and inscribed, showing the sails, the ladder the tube and the lock.

DRINKING VESSELS

BRATINA

Ceremonial covered loving cup found only in Russia, with a small lip and frequently a moral inscription, occasionally richly jeweled or enameled. A very personal cup, used at the owner's funeral.

WINE CUPS

Made in silver, largely in England from about 1550 until glass became fashionable in 1673, their forms copying continental glass styles and familiar to all as the wine glass shapes used ever since. The shallow, wide-mouthed cup was popular early, engraved or punched in a diaper pattern, copying Venetian glass. This is set on a slender baluster stem on a round, slightly domed foot, common to all except the octagonal style with its tapering bowl (chased with stylized flowers) which had cast open brackets below the bowl and above the slim, tapering stem. Less graceful but of fine quality, a beaker-shaped bowl of larger capacity was made *c* 1625–60 and was usually undecorated.

PORRINGER

A low, two-handled covered cup with many uses, owned by every household in Britain *c* 1660–1700;

Tall, slender wine cup, London, 1629

English porringer by
John Sutton, 1675,
its cover reversible
to use as a dish.

Three English
Commonwealth
wine cups, 1649,
their heavy beaker-
shaped bowls set
on a trumpet foot.

Wine cups. *L to R:*
vase-shaped;
footed-beaker type;
shallow
"champagne" type.

103

DRINKING VESSELS

sometimes described as a "caudle" cup (intended for a warm gruel of spiced wine and sugar), a "posset" cup (hot curdled milk with wine or ale and spices), or a two-handled cup (embracing other types of cup). The porringer, although apparently unknown in France, derives from the French "potage," indicating a use for soups, stews, porridge etc. It varies in height from 50–200mm (2–8in) and the larger ones (usually with a matching salver) which hold a gallon or more, could have been used as a tureen, the smaller ones being an individual cup. To start with breadth, measured across the handles, slightly surpassed height; and the characteristically bulged lower half, wherever it was made, was embossed in the Dutch manner, with animals, flowers and birds, repeated on their tightly fitting covers. Early covers had a spool finial (to reverse as a dish, unless *en suite* with their own salver) but the baluster was more usual than other variations. Such porringers were in very thin silver, their decoration, while often amusing, crudely executed, their beaded caryatid handles poorly cast. Chinoiserie decoration (with scroll handles) was used occasionally in the 1680s, when the bulge was beginning to straighten out; caryatid handles were abandoned by 1690, except for those made in Boston, Massachusetts. Coincidentally with these some porringers were quite plain, or with a calyx of acanthus leaves on the lower half, with straight sides and scroll handles. By 1695 height was greater than breadth, flutes and gadrooning were usual and beaded scroll handles began to give way to the substantial scroll or harp handles used with ceremonial cups, which grew in importance from *c* 1700.

In Boston (1680–1700) such cups (never called

American porringer by Joseph Moulton, Newburyport, Mass., *c* 1785.

Quaiche.

porringers there), were often very similar to the English, although the decoration might also be of stylized flowers or geometric design on a matted ground; those from New York (only three survive) are of fine quality with magnificent Dutch engraving. Irish examples are similar to English, but were imaginative in the bulbous period, of fine quality and rather taller *c* 1695. During the late 17th century a two-handled cup with a ten-lobed rim was a Spanish speciality.

AMERICAN PORRINGER

A round, shallow-bowled dish with one pierced flat-lug handle. Early examples had a slightly domed base, sides curving up to a straight lip and simple trefoil-shaped handle; from 1680 the body bellied to an everted lip with a kick-in base and handle piercing varied (largely hearts in Philadelphia but diverse in New York). From *c* 1725 keyhole pattern became universal but, whatever the handle, initials on them demonstrate the family importance of these dishes, owned in quantity by every household. In England similar dishes with a domed base may be wine tasters, or bleeding bowls without the dome, but are more likely to be the lid of a skillet.

QUAICHE

A Scottish two-lugged shallow bowl, made in silver *c* 1660–1725 (later in the provinces), deriving from a wooden staved bowl of ancient origin. Engraved in sections (to represent staves), with outline flowers, usually tulips or roses, but never thistles. Size varying between 90mm ($3\frac{1}{2}$ins) bowl diameter (early 18th), to 190mm ($7\frac{1}{2}$in, late 17th century). Not dissimilar to the French écuelle (see *The Dinner Table*) but without a cover.

An unusual type of porringer with dish cover; Scottish, 1708, and another, London, 1699, fluted, gadrooned and with beaded handles.

PREPARATION & SERVICE

Objects used in the kitchen or prepared there for use on the table.

BOWLS (or Basins)

Made from early times in all countries, for very varied purposes, or for general solid or liquid use. Many defy definition, but although certain characteristics may fit several types, others will show positively what a bowl was not.

A large example of superlative quality and decoration especially if pre-1700, may be a basin separated from its ewer; if it is of greater depth and large, round or oval, but only lightly decorated or plain it may possibly have been a wash basin; when shallow, like an oval meat dish, with one circular notch in the rim, it is a shaving bowl; while a large "punch" type of bowl (see *The Service of Wine*) may have been intended as a Christening bowl, particularly in protestant countries where they were used; covered bowls, about 40% of all originally, were used for hot food or drink, porridge, soup (before 1725 when purpose-made tureens came in), sauce (boats were used from *c* 1720), puddings or stews etc. Many have now lost their covers, adding to the difficulty of identification. Bowls were also used for

Broad, shallow, two-handled bowls made in Augsburg, 1645–50, the left by Hans Lersson, Bergman, Vimmerby, Sweden, *c* 1680.

A New York bowl of the type made nowhere else, by Cornelius Kierstede, who lived 1675–1757.

sweets, spitting, fruit (medium to large, often on a domed pedestal), toiletries, or sugar. Sugar bowls, were made from c 1690 (but seldom between 1740–90 in England) and were covered (slop bowls, from c 1800 were not). After about 1800, when usually a part of a service, they had handles and became ornate everywhere. They were distinguished in Scotland by a flanged scalloped rim, c 1730–50, and were taller proportionately in Ireland, where no cover was used. Sugar bowls were made only from c 1730 in America while Germany largely retained the sugar box, her bowls mostly being larger than elsewhere, heavily embossed and set on three ball feet. Italian bowls, made prolifically, mostly in Venice in the second half of the 18th century, were like a mini-tureen, small, plain, covered and set on four ball and claw, or hoof, feet with very varied knops, becoming pedestal c 1800. French bowls, beautifully decorated in rococo style, were set on a stand very similar to tureens in the Empire period and possibly used as such in smaller families. The écuelle (see *The Dinner Table*), is the most distinctive French bowl.

In New York hemispherical bowls (c 1680–1725), inspired by the Dutch brandy bowl (see below), were

PREPARATION & SERVICE

divided into six panels by chased lines, each division filled by an embossed flower. Set on a decorative stamped rim foot, set slightly higher in later examples, and with two well-cast beaded caryatid handles, these bowls, 180–300mm (7–12in) in breadth, are of superlative quality and made nowhere but New York. Irish bowls took many forms, but their distinctive small circular bowl had an everted rim, sometimes scalloped, and was set on three feet supported by lions masks, shells, or in Cork, human masks; decoration from *c* 1735–80 might consist only of curved or straight incised lines, particularly in Cork and Limerick. Such lines might also be punched, but while punched incisions on the everted rim might occasionally be found from Dublin struck from above, those struck from beneath, giving a convex impression, are a Cork speciality. Irish bowls were often chased with fruit or flowers *c* 1750, but during the 1760s decoration included imaginative farmyard scenes (found also on dish rings, sauce boats and cream jugs). Such themes persisted into the pierced neoclassic period.

BRANDY BOWL

An oval bowl averaging 7–12in in length, with two flat

L : Bowl by Andrew Fogelburg and Stephen Gilbert, London, 1789, beautifully decorated in neoclassic style.

Octagonal bowl by Joseph Clare, London, 1713. Note the thickness of silver.

handles, scrolled or pierced, set on a low rim foot and lightly decorated. Made in Holland in the 17th and early 18th centuries for festive occasions, when raisins soaked in brandy were eaten with a spoon. Smaller bowls with two flat handles were used for serving hot brandy (to drink) in Scandinavia, 17th century.

SWEETMEAT DISHES (Saucers)

Small dishes (up to 150mm/6in diam.) used for many purposes in the 17th century, mainly for mixing sauces at table, or for holding ingredients for them. Round or occasionally oval, in very thin silver, with wavy rims, incised lines and flat shell handles; decoration in England was mainly punched in simple floral patterns. Very popular in Germany where embossed decoration included birds, fruit and flowers. During the 18th century (when Scandinavian examples were set on a capstan foot), they became saucers as we know them, or were used as dishes in an epergne.

CHAFING DISH or BRAZIER

Plate warmer consisting of a bowl, pierced to allow a draft to the charcoal burner inside, with or without a straight wooden handle, held by three or four supports (their ball and claw feet on wooden insulators) which

R: Lobed bowl by Anders Lundquist, Stockholm, 1834.

Hexagonal bowl by Goldsmiths and Silversmiths Co., London, 1910.

PREPARATION & SERVICE

extended above to hold a plate or dish. Most popular in America, c 1680–1750, where straight sides and severe supports became, like the piercing, increasingly graceful with time. A few made in France and England.

SCALDINI

Portable braziers of tureen shape with hinged handles and a flat, perforated top. Made throughout Europe, but particularly in Italy.

DISH RING

Very characteristic item of Irish silver c 1730–1820. Intended, like the modern table mat, to protect polished surfaces from hot dishes, placed in succeeding courses upon the ring. Early examples were spool-shaped, about 190mm (7½in) wide and under 75mm (3in) high, becoming taller and wider at the base by 1750. Decoratively pierced between retaining rims, formally at first, becoming their most enchanting by about 1765, showing Irish scenes with milkmaids, cows, trees, houses, birds, flowers, pigs eating from a trough, the farmer and his dog all amid a background of scrolls and foliage. Becoming symmetrical c 1780, with geometric piercing and solid bands of bright-cut engraving. Very occasionally made elsewhere but essentially Irish.

DISH CROSS

A more adaptable means of keeping hot dishes from the table, popular in England from c 1730–1800. Adjustable arms and legs (in one piece) held any shape or size of dish, kept warm by a central spirit lamp.

DISH COVERS

Used from about 1800 to keep food hot during its journey from kitchen to table. Usually massive and

Irish dish ring, Dublin, 1782, geometrically pierced, with bright cut engraving and a dish ring frame, 1749.

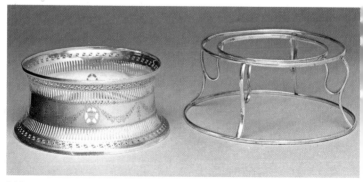

occasionally richly decorated, but more often found only with armorial engraving, a family crest sometimes forming a finial.

SALVERS AND WAITERS

The dividing line between salvers and waiters, on which small objects were presented, is largely a matter of size, waiters never being larger than 23mm (9in) although salvers, up to 275mm (18in) or more, could be less. They evolved from the dish associated with 17th-century porringers and had no handles. In all countries their wide rims were embossed in the Dutch manner. Waiters were often made *en suite* with the salver, or as part of a toilet service. Usually round until *c*1715, shape then being circular, square, oval or polygonal; the waiter more often square with shaped corners. Early 18th-century plain-molded borders

English dish cross.

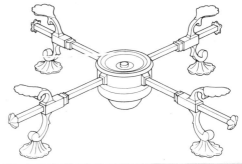

Irish dish ring pierced and chased in their own distinctive rococo form.

PREPARATION & SERVICE

included Chippendale (piecrust) its scrolls and curves popular at all times, rococo shells varying the theme mid century; applied borders with cast chasing in great variety followed current fashion, and piercing was also used from *c*1735–70, when beaded borders became the most usual. From *c*1730, and in a few earlier exceptions, flat chasing surrounded the border, cluttering the surface if not of top quality; this became overall *c*1820; make certain such decoration is contemporary.

Difficult to make and largely produced by specialists, salvers survive in quantity and were well made in Scotland in the early 18th century, flat chasing there becoming coarse by *c*1750. The form followed similar lines everywhere although Italy retained the plain style

Salver with a good 'Chippendale' border and well engraved armorials within a rococo cartouche, London, 1736.

Waiter by John Robinson, London, 1753, one of a set of four.

18th-century American waiter with gadrooned and shaped border and a crest within a rococo cartouche.

PREPARATION & SERVICE

throughout, while Spain, where production was prolific, and Germany were more ambitious in the same idiom. Used as a paten on a trumpet foot in Ireland till *c*1750, an inscription to the Church replacing armorials.

TRAYS

Generally, though not necessarily, larger than the salver and more often oblong or oval, the tray *has handles and no feet*, except in rare transitional cases *c*1775 when handles were used with feet. Developing along similar lines, with borders, flat chasing and armorials from *c*1775; confusion frequently arises because of undue emphasis on size and shape.

SAUCEPANS

Cooking vessels, originally set on a spirit burner, with

R: Tea tray by Hannam & Crouch, London, 1799, reed and bead border and flat chasing within.

Below R: A heavy tray by John Bridge London, 1825.

Tray by Gustavus Byrne, Dublin, 179? reeded handles bright cut engraving

114

PREPARATION & SERVICE

bellied or straight sides, an everted lip and a pouring lip and one straight wooden handle. Small examples were sometimes used for heating brandy. Eighteenth-century examples survive and some may have been made earlier, although the majority date from the early 19th century and on the continent were covered (slip-on covers in France). Small saucepans with a straight wooden handle were for heating brandy.

SKILLET
A 17th century saucepan with three or four legs and a tightly fitting rounded cover with one pierced lug handle, similar to a bleeding bowl or American porringer when separated. Used to prepare hot drinks at table.

COOKING POTS AND PANS
Large saucepans, preserving pans and fish kettles, identical to those of today, were made from the 18th century for kitchen use; plain with engraved armorials.

EGG BOILERS
Small vessels for boiling eggs at table over a spirit lamp, the eggs fitting into an interior frame lifted out by a tall ring handle, c 1790–1820. Occasionally an hour glass for timing was incorporated in the handle; at times made complete with a tray and egg cups or, more rarely, a toast rack.

Below: Silver gilt saucepan, London, 1913.

R: A large saucepan by John Downes, London, 1708, with a small silver gilt pan, Paris, 1809, and an English brandy warmer, London, 1749.

Below C: A silver egg coddler on lampstand, by Hubin & Heath, Birmingham, c 1910

Below R: Egg coddler designed by Christopher Dressler and made by Hubin & Heath, Birmingham, 1878.

PREPARATION & SERVICE

EGG FRAME AND CUPS
Made in the 17th and 18th centuries wherever boiled eggs are served in the shell; the frame for carrying a number of eggs and spoons to table, sometimes complete with salt. Individual egg cups vary from the simple to the magnificent (£5000/$8400 was recently paid for a single cup!).

MENU HOLDERS
Mostly early 20th century, varied and sometimes amusing with an inscribed or decorated front plaque, popular in US.

OTHER COOKING UTENSILS
Skewers survive from *c* 1740 and are keenly collected today, particularly the sharp-edged type, made from *c* 1790 and popular as paper knives. Made in many sizes (matched sets mostly Scottish) with a finial (ring, shell or family crest) designed to assist extraction from the meat. Barding needles, similar to a skewer with a ring handle in scissors style, used to insert bacon under the skin of poultry (or for probing gunshot wounds). Apple corers, as those of today, survive in silver from *c* 1680, lightly engraved. Mote spoons, pierced in the bowl and used for skimming floating tea leaves at table, *c* 1700–90, the long spiked end for cleaning the spout of the teapot. Pastry cutters, rare but attractive and still useful for decorating or trimming pastry. Kitchen peppers, usually cylindrical with a single handle to one side, were for use when the lady visited the kitchen, while muffineers, from *c* 1760, were a form of caster in period and were used for sprinkling spice.

A pair of menu holders by William Comyns, London, 1894.

Straining spoon, London, 1802, and two skewers from sets of four, Dublin 1808, and by Eley and Fearn, London, 1802.

Basting spoon by William Fawdery, London, 1712, with tubular handle and deep bowl.

A silver gilt egg cruet for six by Emes and Barnard, London, 1810.

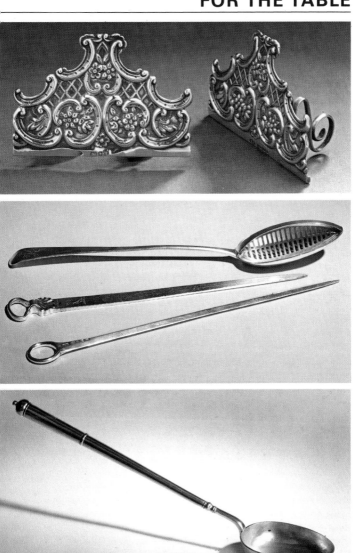

THE DINNER TABLE

Domestic silver in the average family has been put to so many uses that the purpose for which it was made originally is often obscure.

DISHES

Round or oval sideboard dishes were made for display decreasingly until *c*1720, often parcel gilt and highly embossed. In Italy they remained renaissance in style; in Spain, Portugal and Germany they were sometimes very pictorial with a raised central boss; while Antwerp in the late 16th and early 17th centuries was unsurpassed for fine engraving on fairly small octagonal dishes. In England those described as "standing dishes" are footed salvers, originally for use with large porringers. Decoration was confined to borders for serving dishes made as part of a dinner service from *c*1700 and any with an embossed center, whatever their description, were not used for food. Reeded or gadrooned rims are usual in early pieces, decoration following period styles thereafter, a family crest on the upper rim, armorials sometimes found centrally. The

Meat dish with reeded border, Brunswick, 1773; a highly embossed Portuguese display dish, *c*1730; a small dish with raised center, Amsterdam, 1746; and a fluted strawberry dish, Dublin, 1718.

interior depression was usually oval for meat dishes (sometimes with ribbed runnels for gravy from c 1800) and circular for second course dishes, the outer rims of all varying in shape considerably, the smallest were intended as sauceboat stands. Long dishes, for fish, were general throughout continental Europe, but unknown in England.

PLATES

Wooden trenchers were gradually replaced by silver plates from about 1550, survivors mostly dating from c 1700. Decoration was confined to borders and shapes. Made in dozens as part of a matching service, their size decreasing from about 250mm (10in) for meat to 120mm (5in). Fruit plates, usually gilded and embossed with fruit motifs, were rarely made *en suite* with a dinner service.

STRAWBERRY DISHES

Small fluted dishes with scalloped rims forming panels, used for soft fruit in England and Ireland (where most common) c 1700–30, occasionally later, when the shallow sloping sides became steeper and deeper. Usually made in Britannia standard silver and engraved

Three dinner plates, with shaped gadroon border by Martin Guillalme Biennais, Paris, 1809; silver gilt with armorial, English, 1810 and gilt with armorial center by John Luff, 1743.

THE DINNER TABLE

only with armorials, a few being flat-chased in England and Holland.

COMPOSTIERA
An Italian dish for stewed fruit, usually on a salver.

COMPOTES
Standing fruit dish of the 19th century, popular in US.

SCALLOP SHELLS
Used in various forms, particularly by maritime nations, since 2000 BC. Popular as lids for spice boxes (see *The Service of Wine*). Cast dishes in shell form were made for butter, prawns, oysters etc *c* 1720–1830, usually with feet, reaching their superlative and most natural during the rococo period especially fine in France.

CASSEROLE or ENTRÉE DISHES
The word "casserole" derives from the French, describing a cooking pan in which food was subsequently served. Distinguishable from the entrée (a two-handled dish with a variable cover) by a single straight detachable handle, the rounded bowl standing high on a lampstand (from *c* 1725). The entrée dish (from 1770) was sometimes divided inside for vegetables; square, polygonal or pin-cushion (with incurving sides) in shape, these shallow dishes were placed over spirit lamps until the 19th century, when a hot water container was incorporated underneath, France continuing with lamps on tall claw supports until mid century.

Entrée dish with gadrooned rims, English, 1819.

THE DINNER TABLE

MAZARINE

A pierced plate for use in a serving dish, allowing juices to drain. Usually oval, with fine engraving and piercing indicating fish as a principal use. Made from the late 17th century, but usually in Sheffield plate after 1780.

TUREENS

The large soup tureen evolved from the French pottery "terrine" and it was everywhere one of the most important objects made for the table. First known *c*1720, when averaging about 300mm (12in) in breadth; usually oval; set on four good cast feet, claw, hoof, shell etc, with masks; handles (scroll, drop or ring) and imposing covers with variable finials. Becoming more richly decorated (and increasing in size) with rococo, when some superlative tureens were

One of a pair of entrée dishes and covers by Paul Storr, 1817, and two from a set of four to match by Phillip Rundell, London, 1820, all with detachable handles.

A scallop shell in the style of Paul Storr, London, 1972, and another (*R*) from Salamanca, *c*1780.

THE DINNER TABLE

made, particularly in France and Italy (where 18th-century simplicity was forgotten). Handles, feet and covers were heavy with fruit, vegetables and superbly modeled figures, animal or human in perfect balance, some quite plain examples appearing coincidentally (usually provincial), animal and human figures or groups on the lid in Germany being of great size and quality. By mid century they are usually found on a stand (always used in France although often lost); pedestal bases largely replace feet c 1770, now in classical shapes with applied motifs; becoming gracefully light in England where boat-shaped, with high, loop handles, often with fluted bodies and stands, sometimes built up to a platform to increase height; height now frequently greater than width, always so in Scandinavia where shape is normally circular. Tureens were rare in America and Canada, but some were made in the French Empire style from about 1810, although lacking French grandeur. In France, massive and superbly decorated within the style, the tureen was sometimes dwarfed by its great stand, while retaining perfect harmony and balance. In England they have a circular form based on the Warwick Vase, with ornament increasing until c 1820 after which over

English tureen with animal crest handle, London, 1755.

Bottom R: Dutch Tureen and cover on a partially-fluted stand by V. C. Beurnkem, Amsterdam, 1764.

Soup tureen and cover by Paul de Lamerie, 1747, incorporating all that is finest in English rococo design and workmanship.

THE DINNER TABLE

German Tureen, Hanover, 1770.

Bottom L : One of a pair of soup tureens and covers by Waterhouse, Hodson & Co., Sheffield, 1829.

French ecuelle by Paul Soulaine, 1747, its lug handles cast and pierced.

ornamentation swamped line and balance everywhere. Late examples were sometimes set on feet.

ECUELLES

Shallow circular covered bowls with two flat, lug handles, cast and chased or pierced, c 1660–1780. A French speciality, 175–190mm (7–7½in) across, but occasionally made by Huguenots in England, Italy, America and Canada (until 1750) and more frequently in Germany where they were very slightly larger. They were low and plain with almost flat covers, decorated with cut card applications in the 17th century, a hinged ring, scroll or coiled snake handle on the cover which becomes domed in the 18th century, its height increasing with time and interest centering on its decoration while bodies mostly remained plain. They were set on a silver stand from about 1733, when a pineapple finial was the most usual, with the lugs usually embossed and very varied. Early German écuelles were set on small button feet but on claw supports in the mid 18th century.

SAUCEBOATS

The earliest sauceboats were double-lipped on an oval base, made in superb quality silver with a molded wavy rim decorated only with armorials particularly c 1715 in England. This shape was used again with rococo decoration, particularly in France and Germany, but

THE DINNER TABLE

rarely in England. The character of the boats, with a lip at either end squared off by a handle on each side, made it difficult to pour from them.

The more familiar boat with one handle opposite a single lip, came in *c* 1725. This type was usually set on a molded base until *c* 1740 and on three or four cast feet thereafter, although not invariably. These boats were very fanciful and highly important in rococo, occasionally with dolphin feet, but more often having a pedestal base forming a platform encrusted with marine life in every shape and form, a few small crustaceans and shells sometimes clinging to the boat itself, otherwise confined to waves and ripples or conventional scrolls and foliage. Handles were formed as marine birds, beautiful or grotesque; griffins or other figures, human or animal, the body sometimes shell shaped. English examples, comparable with the best made in France continued until *c* 1765 when sauce tureens replaced them, and to the mid 19th century elsewhere, mostly on a pedestal foot, heavily decorated in French Empire style.

English sauceboats The most common type *c* 1740–70 with leaf capped flying scroll handle and wavy edge. A heavier type of the same period with animal head to the handle and gadrooned edge, and a high quality type on a pedestal base, 1745.

One of a pair of sauceboats with four 'caterpillar' legs, by Paul de Lamerie, 1742.

One of a pair of Victorian sauceboats by Robert Garrard, London, 1831.

One of a pair of gadrooned sauceboats by Smith and Sharp, London, 1776.

THE DINNER TABLE

Irish examples of the mid 18th century are distinctive, being generally both wider and flatter, with a broad lip, three legs (with rare exceptions), lion's masks above shell feet from *c* 1740, with exotic birds occasionally from *c* 1750, or human masks in Cork and Limerick. Handles were three scroll *c* 1740, with flying scroll, dolphins etc as alternatives by 1750. Body decoration consisted of typically Irish embossing, mostly scrolling foliage, flowers or fruit among which birds might be found; wavy everted rims flat-chased in the Irish manner. The incised lines and punched rim sometimes found on bowls occurring only rarely, usually in Cork and Limerick after rococo had passed. The punching is from beneath in Cork, a speciality of the city, but usually from above in Dublin. This punching was also used in America, *c* 1770, but sauceboats there were uncommon.

SAUCE TUREENS

Vessels evolved from the sauceboat *c* 1765 and soon made as smaller replicas of the boat-shaped soup tureen, usually as a part of a dinner service. Rare outside England, they follow the styles of successive soup tureens.

Neo-classic sauce tureen, London, 1782.

PAP BOAT

A plain boat-shaped vessel with a lip but no handle or feet, *c* 1710–1830. Said to be for infant feeding, a messy possibility. In Canada they may have held Holy Water for baptism.

ARGYLE

A cylindrical or baluster-covered heat retaining vessel for gravy, with a long spout. Heated by an outer hot water jacket or by a hot bar inserted in an inner tube, *c* 1765–1800.

SALTS

The medieval great salt was of prime social importance in England, placed on the table before the host, and the most important guests grouped around him. Many also had compartments for spice, but these great sculptures were of no more practical use than the "hour-glass" salt, peculiar to England *c* 1480–1525; the architectural salts made in all countries during the 16th century; the "bell" salt, *c* 1580–1620 (made only in England); pedestal salts up to 560mm (22in) high, sometimes with a steeple in England between *c* 1590–1610.

European salts of similar period were of less social importance but greater practicability; some were magnificent, particularly in Italy, where horizontal salts of superlative workmanship were exemplified by Cellini's famous gold salt of 1543, with its glorious figure modeling. Quite small examples were also made, particularly in late-16th-century Venice. Holland also used figures effectively (from *c* 1620), the accessible salt container strikingly incorporated into the marine design. Neither Germany nor France featured salts, but French exceptions were square or cylindrical with Limoges enamel plaques, while Germany (where they were mostly small and useful) made a few of the great architectural types. Spain incorporated cabochon enamels on cylindrical salts peculiar to them, with steep, domed covers, and those of Portugal were encrusted with marine motifs. The spool-shaped pulley salt developed in England from the base of the bell salt from *c* 1625, with three or four scrolls rising above it on which a plate was placed in lieu of a cover. Decorated only occasionally, these continued until family dining gained popularity over the Great Hall, *c* 1660. Several fine American salts were made in this form before 1700.

Trencher salts, tiny individual containers raised from a single thin sheet of silver, had long been used

THE DINNER TABLE

additionally to put by each man's place, surviving in England from c 1600 (earlier on the continent, particularly Germany), when they were circular or triangular, soon developing in many shapes, sometimes with a flattened concave curve. Rope borders or ridged sides to a flattened convex line (c 1660) were popular in Europe, particularly Holland, and used with a gadrooned molded base in England, c 1680–1700, when a taller spool with gadrooned edge is found. Considerable overlapping of styles is found at all times, the octagonal oblong, with concave stepped sides and simple moldings, plain in England but applied with medallions, masks etc in Germany, being common 1700–40; like all small simple salts these were made in sets.

Another development from the spool was the circular bowl on a molded spreading foot, c 1725–45, either plain or more often applied with a calyx of acanthus leaves with a chased and molded base. The bulbous "cauldron" salt with an everted rim set on three or four feet, c 1720–60, was popular everywhere, a blue glass liner sometimes used on the continent, although interiors were gilded against salt erosion from about 1730; hoof feet were a feature to start with, then scroll, lion's mask and paw or shell, the rim notched inside; forms were similar in Germany and Russia, but with national style decoration. Some magnificent cast examples were made in this form from c 1730, with dolphin or other marine legs, decoration increasing over the next two decades, the bowl heavily embossed, in rococo motifs, the everted rim with shells. In England Chinese rococo was also used, but German styles remained plain. In exotic rococo the shell was mostly used as the salt container, sometimes quite simply as a cockle shell on three tiny scroll or shell feet, although the rococo salt could be totally fantastic, particularly in France where a shell container appears somewhere amid an exuberance of rolling marine motifs; others (mostly by François-Thomas Germain) incorporate children, scrolls and shells quite delightfully. A "cauldron" form placed *on a low rim foot* with varied decoration, came over a century later, c 1860–90.

The classical revival brought in the pierced oval straight-sided salt, c 1760, a blue glass liner shining through. Scroll piercing was used at first, then geometric with swags, ribbons, urns or medallions overlaid, with stamped ball and claw feet; very popular

Some of the wide variety of shapes of salt ranging over 200 years from the simple triangular trencher to the pierced circular salt with a glass liner and including spool, cauldron and octagonal forms and the pulley shape (shown top right).

From 1620

1625 (Dutch)

c 1625 (Dutch)

1625–60

c 1635

c 1685–95

c 1700

1710–25

1710–40

c 1710–30

c 1730–60

1790–1800

c 1810

German   1810–30

c 1820

1830–50

133

THE DINNER TABLE

throughout Europe and America, as was the boat shape (c 1780–1800) similar but with curved, beaded or reeded rims, sometimes fluted; plain or with bright cut engraving and only a little or no cutting. A boat shape, with high loop handles, set on a pedestal foot, was made at the same period and until 1805. Italy continued with classical shapes and decoration until mid 19th century, classicism becoming fanciful from 1820, incorporating motifs such as outstretched wings, single-leg swans and human figures in fantastic tableaux, by which time French Empire style was affecting the majority of European goldsmiths. A rounded oblong on four ball feet followed c 1805–15, and a straight-sided, circular, classical salt, which was set on feet with regular piercing and a blue glass liner was made c 1830–50, but the 19th century was generally one of revival styles, the cauldron with heavy

The best of revival work in a set of four salts by Robert Garrard, London, 1863.

Bell Salt, 1601, an exclusively English type.

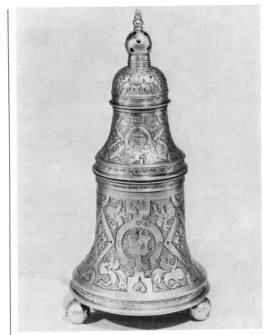

Gilded salt, pierced with blue glass lining, 1740; plain circular salt on a spreading foot, 1693, and a gadrooned low salt, 1846.

THE DINNER TABLE

gadroons, lions' or sphinx masks; vines, grapes etc gradually overtaken by grotesque bad taste, although both England and France also reverted to the delights of rococo, with children on encrusted rocks holding out shells; donkeys with pannier salt holders and other imaginative frivolities.

CASTERS

Tall cylinders made for sprinkling sugar, spices and other condiments; originated in France, c 1650, reaching England c 1670 and New York 1695. They were produced in sets of three (more often single in Scotland), the largest for sugar, with one "blind" or unpierced, for dry mustard. The "lighthouse" caster (until c 1705) had straight sides and a high, flattened pierced dome, fixed by a bayonet joint and with fairly large foliate piercing (for coarse sugar), gadroons, rope moldings or occasional cut card work being the only decoration beyond armorials. Quality of piercing and fit of cover are of prime importance in all casters. The pear

Three casters. *L to R:* 1709, 1785 (by Hester Bateman) and 1726.

shape was used from *c* 1700, with a molded rib usually encircling the widest part of the body which is set on a molded foot, the cover higher and more rounded with a baluster finial and fine piercing; it is sometimes octagonal and usually undecorated but cut card is occasionally found on early examples. This form evolved rather than changed, a shoulder developing which quickly moved down the body forming a bulge which increased in ratio to the ever slimming, incurved waist above, to become a definite shoulder. Decoration, even during the rococo period, was generally restrained, but within national styles, although German goldsmiths used animal forms in their own manner. Casters lost their place to sugar bowls *c* 1770 in England, but on the continent continued in addition to bowls without great change.

Novelties:
Champagne cork
pepper mill,
Birmingham, 1903;
Birds pepper and
salt, 1919,
Tower pepper,
Birmingham, 1890.

PEPPERS
Small casters, usually one of a set of three. "Bun" peppers (from *c* 1725) had a flattened top (kitchen

THE DINNER TABLE

peppers see *Preparation and Service for the Table*).
Many variations were made in the 19th century
following no set style.

MUSTARD POTS

Dry mustard was kept in a caster *c* 1680–1750,
although separate vase-shaped pots were also known
in England from the early 18th century and ovoid forms
on a gadrooned pedestal base (copied in New York
c 1725) in Holland, while pots on a high pedestal foot
with a high scroll handle were prevalent in France. They
became barrel or tankard shape *c* 1750–80, gilded
inside and with a flat or domed lid, and a drum shape
was made from *c* 1760 with straight sides and scroll
handle: these were pierced in attractive variety, first
scrolling then geometric, sometimes with bright-cut
engraving. Oval and boat-shaped pots were also made.
Their lids sometimes flat at first, but more often with a
dome which gained height until *c* 1800, and a finial and
a thumbpiece that were as varied as the cutting. From
c 1775–90 they are sometimes vase-shaped on a
pedestal foot; beaded borders appear 1775–85,
thereafter they follow salt styles and are often fantastic.

Large cruet frame
for three casters and
five bottles,
London, 1763.

CRUET FRAME

Originally a silver frame to hold bottles for wine and water for the communion service, continuing as such in period to the present time on the continent, in great variety. Silver-topped glass bottles for oil and vinegar, sometimes with handles, were held in a cruet frame in England from *c* 1715 and when complete with three casters were called a Warwick cruet. Varying in decoration from the simple to the magnificent, these frames consisted basically of retaining rings above a tray on feet, frequently with a tall central ring handle. After about 1770, when the trays became boat-shaped,

Cruet frame with three casters and two bottles, London, 1752.

Mustard pots, plain drum by Eliza Godfrey, *c* 1755, and barrel shaped by Henry Chawner, 1792; all London.

THE DINNER TABLE

casters were also of glass; the form became oval by 1800 when any number of bottles for soy and other sauces were included.

EPERGNE

A centerpiece frame on which several detachable dishes or baskets were mounted, usually rising to a larger central basket; early examples sometimes incorporated candleholders. They were made *c*1715–1800 for fruits, nuts, sweetmeats etc, decoration being in period; lavish in rococo and well suited to the Chinese style, *c*1740, particularly with pagodas.

CENTERPIECE

A large object placed to catch the eye on the center of the table from the earliest time (the nef, great salt, figural tazze etc), either purely decorative or incorporating a purpose, such as candelabra or épergnes. French goldsmiths excelled with particularly fine, imaginative rococo forms. The centerpiece was a great outlet for the 19th-century sculptural goldsmith who recreated historic, sporting or other occasions, depicting every detail in monumental pieces weighing 3kg

Gilded centerpiece with four light brackets by J. W. Storey and William Elliott, London, 1811.

Silver epergne with cut glass bowls, by Matthew Boulton, Birmingham, 1817.

THE DINNER TABLE

(1000ozs) or more. Modern goldsmiths have now brought the centerpiece to its finest form, variable in purpose and adjustable in shape, according to need.

PLATEAUX

Long galleried trays for the banqueting table on which all the appertenances of a dinner service could be stood; made (but rarely all in silver) in England and America early in the 19th century, sometimes magnificently sculptured at the ends and rising to a monumental centerpiece or épergne.

An equestrian centerpiece by Robert Garrard, London, 1851.

THE TEA TABLE

The elegance of Georgian living was personified in the ritual of the tea table and objects used for it have long been favorites among collectors.

COFFEE AND CHOCOLATE POTS

The most important difference between pots made for coffee and those for chocolate was an opening under the detachable or swivel finial on the lid of the chocolate pot, necessary for the insertion of a molinet, or stirring rod, with which to whip up the thick liquid. Often dual-purposed, these pots were made throughout Europe and America from *c*1680–1740, when jugs replaced them for chocolate. With rare vase-shaped exceptions (pre 1700) chocolate pots mirrored those made for coffee without further distinguishing points.

Early English coffee pots had a conical lid with a straight spout, a cylindrical body and a rounded handle that might, until 1720, be set opposite the spout, or at right angles to it (when a thumbpiece is also found). This position persisted on the continent in conjunction with a straight-turned wooden handle, a feature never popular in England or America, where styles mostly followed the English from 1670.

Top L to R: German neo-classical, *c*1790; French coffee pot, 1750–60; French chocolate pot 1750–70; *bottom:* German coffee pot, 1815; English conical coffee pot, *c*1680–1700.

THE TEA TABLE

By 1700, when the spout curved, the English lid was rounded, sometimes fluted and had a baluster finial; handle and spout joints were frequently strengthened by cut card applications and armorial engraving (the only decoration used before 1730) was placed opposite the handle, whatever its position. Styles overlapped but the cylindrical body persisted until *c* 1735 and was often polygonal after 1700; curved facetted spouts, often cast with a hinged flap or "duck's head" were usual after 1710; wooden handles were double scrolled and lids gradually flattened until *c* 1725.

The pear shape came in gradually from about 1730, the straight sides at first merely rounding in to a molded base; this "tucked under" pot was made until *c* 1755, its body curving to pear form increasingly until the late 1760s, again with a domed lid. English pots *c* 1730–40 might be flat-chased or embossed thereafter until *c* 1760, but flamboyant rococo was rare and then often in Chinese style. Cast spouts were frequently the most decorated part of the pot, leaf-capped or terminating in a bird's head, richly scrolled near the joint. Irish pots

Octagonal coffee pot by John Jackson, London, 1709, and another of much greater size but exceptional quality, London, 1758.

were of fine quality and typically embossed with living creatures hiding among the scrolls.

The pear shape originated in France where the pot was usually set on three slim legs (general throughout Europe and not unknown in Ireland) and had a small pouring lip, more suitable to the thick Turkish coffee they favored; it tended to be somewhat squat with a flattish lid surmounted by a leaf or berry finial; swirling flutes were typical and handles were either straight and at right angles, or curved; rococo decoration, when used, was universally restrained, although Scandinavian pots (very squat and so asymmetrical in form as to appear lop-sided) could be richly embossed, while Russian and Venetian pots were oriental in style, frequently incorporating niello. With the exception of small details, such as the cartwheel mótif in the handle sockets of Maltese pots, variations were slight.

By 1770 the coffee pot had grown higher and slimmer, the vase shape with a tall slim spool-like neck above a shoulder evolving from it, with high loop handles; restrained decoration consisted of little more than fluting or swags and husks, beaded borders of

Conical chocolate pot with removable finial, by Samuel Wastell, London, 1703 and a French chocolate pot with hinged finial, 1774.

THE TEA TABLE

foliage, occasionally with medallions and other classical motifs; gadroons might be used as edging and bright-cut engraving was usual from *c* 1780. These pots were made increasingly as part of a tea and coffee set, many coffee pots doing double duty as hot water jugs; such vessels nearly always had the wide pouring lip of a covered jug, the true pot retaining the long curved spout. This elegant line was best portrayed in England and America, and the fine examples made in Philadelphia, often incorporating their own distinctive gallery, which was sometimes used around the wide shoulders, curved in to a comparatively narrow neck above, this neck itself was surmounted by a taller spool lid with an urn finial. Such pots have a trumpet foot which is set on a square base, the only straight line among the convex and concave curves.

Nineteenth-century coffee pots, pear-shaped and often on feet, were comparatively squat, usually following the lines of tea sets, decorated *en suite* (often with restraint) and frequently standing on a spirit lamp. They were also made in a straight-sided form, set on a lamp in England (where they are known as a biggin) and these were popular in Scandinavia and Germany.

Octagonal Queen Anne tea and coffee pots, each on its own stand, by Joseph Ward, London, 1719.

146

TEAPOTS

Dutch ships first brought tea to Holland in 1610 and the vast majority of all continental silver for tea now offered for sale is Dutch. Russia next had tea (1618), then France (1648), but French teapots are rare as the French preferred coffee and chocolate; England first tasted tea in 1650 and America soon after. The first Dutch teapots were shaped like a Chinese wine pot, an hexagonal egg-shape with matted decoration, a form preceded in England only by a tall conical "coffee" pot, large despite the price of tea which dictated sparing use from a very small pot. In England this ovoid shape (which was taken up with little variation in New York *c* 1700) was (*c* 1700–25) transformed into the Queen Anne pear shape by curving its lines in below the domed lid, adding a baluster finial and a beautifully shaped wooden handle, very occasionally set at right angles, and a facetted, shaped spout tapering towards a hinged duck's head. Such pots, were often octagonal after 1710 and decorated only with armorials or occasionally cut card; height increased slightly with time. Styles varied extraordinarily little between countries, but these important pots, set upon a lamp

L: Newcastle teapot by Isaac Cookson 1745, nearer in style to the Scottish transitional pot than the conventional English bullet pot, but with a curved spout.

C: The inverted pear-shaped teapot was rare in England but was made *c* 1750–60.

R: Pear-shaped Queen Anne tea pot, Scottish. Note the hinged spout.

THE TEA TABLE

stand originally, are almost invariably of superb quality.

The bullet teapot became popular *c* 1720, although occasionally made earlier; round, flattish on top and set on a low molded rim base (a little higher towards 1740) it had a straight tapering spout with a bright cut mouth and a curved wooden handle standing well out from silver sockets. Such pots might be polygonal before 1730; spouts curved and were often facetted from *c* 1740, but decoration, other than flat chasing over the shoulders, was rare until the form was dying out in the 1750s (60s in Scotland). Such pots had almost flat lids, while the lid of the Scottish bullet completes a full circle and is further distinguished (after a short transitional period) by standing up above a spreading base; its handle is ample and high and before 1730 engraving might surround the shoulders, spilling over the sides, or flat chasing thereafter, the cut biting deeper into the metal as time progressed. Very small teapots, in either pear shape from *c* 1702, or bullet from 1713, were made in Ireland to 1730, but any Irish teapots between 1730–80 were from Cork.

Bullet teapots in the contemporary English style were made in Boston from *c* 1735, but not New York, which continued with the pear shape in somewhat high, narrow form. The inverted pear shape (*c* 1750–70), was rare in England but such pots were popular in America, particularly Boston, although also made in Philadelphia (where the stepped foot was somewhat higher) and New York (lower). It had a cast, curved, facetted, leaf-capped spout emerging from the upper bulge and decoration, in restrained rococo, spills half way down the sides from the slightly domed cover and shoulders. In England the spout might end in a bird's head and lid decoration was sometimes repeated on the foot. Overall decoration was very rare but when contemporary clear spaces divide the embossed scrolls and flowers, 19th-century additions normally having a matted background. Continental examples differed little, a Portuguese teapot, *c* 1745 (on accompanying salver) exemplifying their high standards.

Neoclassical teapots, from about 1765, were circular drums with flat top and base, becoming straight sided oval by 1780, oval with boat-shaped upper outline (frequently on a stand) by 1790 and in varied straight-sided shapes (generally based on the rectangle) by 1800. All had a straight tapering spout emerging from near the base; flat lids, either hinged or loose,

148

18th- and 19th-century teapots. *(Top to bottom and L to R):* Inverted pear, 1760; English or American, fluted boat shape, 1785–1800; Dutch 1770; Danish 1777; English neo-classical 1790–1805; Continental 1800; Victorian, Chinese style 1845.

THE TEA TABLE

becoming domed *c* 1790, when usually part of a service. Decorated with beaded edges alone, or neo-classic engraving bright-cut from *c* 1780. Fundamentally these styles prevailed with few variations in Europe but important differences appeared in the US. In Boston there were three basic types: the drum shape which was considerably higher than in England, surmounted by a spool-shaped collar, with a stepped rounded lid and high cone finial, beaded at all edges; the oval pot, its straight sided body almost as high as broad, which had a centrally domed cover raised by a reeded step, surmounted by a high finial and surrounded by a flattish border; or an oval-bodied pot with broad fluting (a Paul Revere speciality). All have tapering straight spouts and carved handles. Philadelphia made two types: broader oval pots without the collar but with a gently sloping lid (not domed) and beading; and tall urn-shaped pots on a high pedestal, with curved spout and urn finial, similar to their coffee pot of the period (more squat to start with but becoming higher, more elegant and less distinguishable) usually part of a service. (Heavier, more ornate and lacking the elegance, the 19th-century pot is based, broadly, on this shape.) In New York, where bright-cut engraving excelled, the oval pot had had an extra-long, straight spout and a stepped, domed cover, but the shaped rectangle with concave cut corners was more usual and had a round or octagonal spool-shaped

Tea urn made 176 and decorated in the Chinese style.

R. below : Teapot made in China for export to Britain, *c* 1875.

Oval cylindrical tea pot by Jas Mitchellson, Edinburgh, 1722; early bullet by Edmund Pearce, 1714 and a silver gilt teapot, Augsburg, 1751–3

dome set centrally on a one-stepped lid; the spout was usually straight, but sometimes curved gently.

The 19th-century revivals and mixed styles were preceded by a compressed oval or round pot (c 1800–20), sometimes fluted, characterized by a sunken cover protected by a raised collar. An oblong pot on four ball feet followed (jumbled styles contemporarily) and the lobed melon (c 1830) also appeared and led to many variations as design deteriorated. Thereafter any shape, size or combination of decorative forms might be found, usually as part of a full service.

TEA or COFFEE URNS

Large receptacles for dispensing quantities of hot water effortlessly by means of a tap set low in the body. Immediately popular on introduction c 1760, their charcoal burners soon being replaced by a heated iron bar inserted into an inner tube. Some early gourd-shaped urns were decorated in exuberant rococo, cast, pierced and embossed, although the majority in neo-classic lines with typical embellishment. Although some heavy but good urns were made in the early 19th century they were mostly in Sheffield plate after 1790, when globular in form and set on a spirit burner; like the Russian samovar which makes tea on the same principle, the massive tea machine, with its three round urns which developed from this, was also rare in silver. The French combined silver with ormulu in elegant

THE TEA TABLE

classic forms, but although many follow these general trends, no heating arrangements appear on a number from Germany, Holland and Ireland (first known dated 1698) which have two or three spigot taps and were possibly intended for cold drinks. The very distinctive Scottish urn of the 1730s is also unheated; of pure egg form, this is set on three tall cabriole legs with serpent handles.

TEA KETTLES

Large kettles on a spirit lamp (c 1690–1760) were used for refilling the teapot and were made in virtually the same body styles as the teapot, with swing handles and a wide flat base. After the plain pear-shape, kettles generally carried a little more decoration than teapots (rococo sometimes exuberantly), most of it concentrated on the frieze surrounding the three-legged stand which originally stood on a salver until insulated feet (shell the most common) obviated the need for it. When the tea urn became popular c 1760, few kettles

Flat-chased tea urn in neo-classic style by Henry Chawner, London, 1790.

L: Bullet tea kettle by John White, London, 1734 on stand of 1737.

R: Melon-shaped tea kettle on burner stand by John Chartier, London, 1735.

THE TEA TABLE

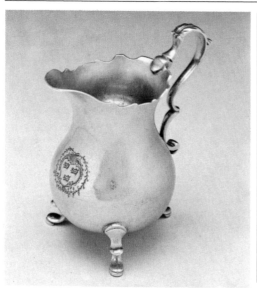

An American three legged cream jug, c 1740.

A herd of cow creamers by John Schuppe, London 1757–65.

embossed cream
at, London,
53.

ightly embossed
tch cream jug,
49; one with a
nched rim and set
a pedestal base,
ndon, 1771, and
eproduction pear
ape, Birmingham,
06.

were made (except in Holland) although sometimes included in an early 19th-century tea service.

CREAM (or MILK) JUGS

Although noted by a Dutchman in Canton in 1655 milk was not used in tea in Europe before the early 18th century (cream *c* 1780). The earliest purpose-made jugs (*c* 1715) were almost 750mm (3in) high, pear-shaped with a cast scroll handle, small applied lip and a low rim foot (growing higher *c* 1730). A few cast helmet type jugs in strange, fanciful forms were also made *c* 1720–40 (somewhat similar in Scandinavia *c* 1760–70, but rounder and more attractive). Cream jugs generally inspired many individual variations, including Paul de Lamerie's foreshortened "sauce-boat" type *c* 1735–45 and the Scandinavian sauce-boat creamer of the rococo period (to 1775) lower and wider and set on three leaf feet; cow creamers, realistically bovine in shape, were made in Holland *c* 1740–50 and from 1757–68 in England, where they were exclusively the work of John Schuppe, himself believed to have been a Dutchman. The milk goes into the cow under the saddle and pours out through the mouth, flies on the nose or udder adding realism.

THE TEA TABLE

The pear shape continued to about 1770 (weight of silver deteriorating) set on three hoof feet, increasingly from *c* 1730 with shell knuckles; a wavy everted rim incorporated a broad pouring lip. Such jugs were embossed tastefully with rococo flowers etc mid century. In Ireland the lip was always wider, helmet-shaped (without the pear's waist) and with a molded band encircling the center (rare in England). Such jugs *c* 1750–80 (when slightly less broad) might be embossed with all the charm of Irish "farmyard" rococo, or plain (to 1770), with lion's mask and paw feet; hoof feet with shell knuckles or human mask (usually Cork or Limerick) the third foot placed *under the lip* in Ireland, but *under the handle* in England. American jugs followed the English form.

A brief transitional period in England (*c* 1770) saw the pear shape, embossed or plain, set on a high pedestal foot, but by 1775 (until *c* 1805) English goldsmiths, like those of the majority of western countries, adopted a tall helmet shape which first appeared in Holland about 1765. It had a beaded or applied rim, decorated in neoclassic style, a circular foot set on a square base (itself on four ball feet in Scandinavia), and a high loop handle. A variation of

George II cream boat by Dorothy Mills and Thomas Sarbitt, London, 1747.

Very fine tea caddy with a hinged lid, embossed in the Chinese style, by Samuel Pitts, London, 1761.

this form is vase-shaped and in Ireland has a spool neck. The broad, flat-bottomed type (c 1775–1805) was virtually the last individual style, cream jugs thereafter being made as part of a service. Creamers were rare in France and Germany.

CREAM PAILS

Straight sided hooped buckets with a swing handle, c 1730 in England, called a "piggin" in Ireland c 1775, with a vertical heart-shaped handle; in France, c 1770, they had a flat slip-on cover and three decorative legs; the sides became tapered and shaped by 1770 (Ireland 1790) when they were usually pierced, with a blue glass liner.

TEA CADDIES

Canisters in which to keep tea, the word derived from the Malay word "Kati," a measure of weight. Plain oval, rectangular or octagonal with straight sides (c 1700–25), the flat top was surmounted by a "bun" domed cover, itself used as a measure (tea inserted through a sliding panel underneath). A very similar toilet canister had chinoiserie flat chasing in England (1680s) and a ring carrying handle in Germany (from 1660). A rectangular box type (c 1715–50) had hinged or pull-off lids, its sides beginning to bulge and

Vase shaped caddies, Dutch, 1751, and embossed with flowers, 1752, by Samuel Taylor, specialist caddy maker, London.

THE TEA TABLE

shoulders to round by 1720, these had molded edges and finial (a bun cover decreasing to 1725). Caddies were usually made in sets of two or three after 1740 (sometimes before), and kept in a lockable silver mounted case. Dutch revivals were popular in the early 19th century. From c1745–70 shapes varied enormously, but included the pear shape, like a fore-shortened caster, with a bun finial; bombé or square boxes made to look like tea chests, the quality of the embossed rococo decoration (often in Chinese style in England) invariably high. Caddies themselves had locks from 1770–1800 when the general form was oval; a flat cover with varied finial at first, domed from c1790; often fluted or with shaped corners, and light neoclassic engraving, bright-cut from about 1780; urn-shaped with applied or embossed classical decoration, or vase-shaped with a spool neck and high loop handles were less popular. Oblong caddies from c1800 varied in shape, sometimes being set on legs. Most of those made outside Britain are Dutch, in similar styles.

SUGAR BOWLS

Small, round covered bowls were made for sugar from the late 17th century (1730 in America), the cover was

Sugar bowls, *L to R*, with handles, 1838; circular, 1729; tall urn shape Philadelphia, 1790 flat chased with reversible cover (to use as spoon tray), 1733.

surmounted by a rim and reversible for use as a spoon tray by 1715 (cups then had no saucers). They were occasionally polygonal and usually decorated only with armorials in America and England (where replaced by caddies 1740–90), returning as part of a tea set only. Continuing elsewhere they had a distinctive flanged and scalloped rim in Scotland c 1730–50, no cover in Ireland, and were always decorated in national style in France and Holland, but never excessively. The bowl grew taller, gradually becoming vase-shaped by 1760, often with a swing handle, sometimes pierced, with a blue glass liner, decorated in classic forms. America excelled, the urn gaining height by the use of tall spool covers, sometimes galleried in Philadelphia; styles followed those of the tea service in the 19th century, often being ornate and two-handled.

SUGAR BASKETS

The vase-shaped pierced sugar bowl with a swing handle, overlaid with festoons etc (c 1760) became boat-shaped c 1785, more often solid, sometimes with broad flutes or shaped rims and decorated with bright-cut engraving.

'Batwing' sugar basket by Henry Chawner, 1793; Slop bowl by Peter and William Bateman, 1806, both London.

THE TEA TABLE

SPOON TRAY
A small oval dish (or the ringed lid of a sugar bowl) on which tea drinkers could lay their spoons after stirring, c1700–60. Plain at first, then scalloped like a strawberry dish (often Irish) or otherwise decorated around the rim (often shaped), sometimes set on four feet. Similarities occasionally cause confusion, but the snuffer tray (see *Lighting*) although of similar shape, had a side handle; while a pen tray was larger and made only from c1770.

SLOP BOWLS
Small bowls without covers into which slops could be tipped or on which tea strainers rested.

HOT WATER JUGS
Jugs on a small spirit lamp made to keep water hot from c1790, replacing urns in the family (see also *The Service of Wine*).

TEA CUPS
Silver cups and saucers without handles were abandoned as impracticable for hot drinks c1715 and replaced by porcelain cups, sometimes silver mounted; in Norway, c1730, these might also have a silver cover.

TREMBLEUSE
A silver frame, on a saucer, often foliate, for holding a porcelain teacup or glass. French in origin but extensively made in Genoa, c1750–70, and in Germany in magnificent rococo form.

TEA or COFFEE SERVICES
Individual objects for the tea table had been made to go well with each other from the start, but services were not made as such before 1785 except occasionally for royal use, or in Scotland during the 1730s. They then became popular everywhere, often complete with a tray, slop basin and hot water jug on a burner stand. Kettles, although out of period, and urns (losing popularity c1790), might also be found. In period form to c1825 (1850 in France), after which any form might appear, covered profusely in jumbled ornament or (occasionally) tastefully restrained.

BASKETS
Whether described as for bread, cake, fruit or sweetmeats (smaller and possibly separated from an epergne) baskets have been decorative, varied and superlatively pierced since the late 16th century. They survive prolifically in all countries from c1730, generally in oval form, when swing handles (not used early) were joined to pierced, almost upright, sides with

Silver gilt rococo form trembleuse with engraved gla by Andreas Schneider, Augsburg, 1753–

Bottom R: A 4-piec tea and coffee set b Emes and Barnard, London, 1820:

Neo-classical tall covered jug by John Schofield, London, 1790.

THE TEA TABLE

an everted rim by figures, animals, birds etc; they have a flat base and are usually engraved with armorials. By 1740 sides were slightly sloping, the angle increasing *c* 1750, and beautifully cast feet were joined by a pierced frieze, which by 1750 stood out on their own. Simulated basket work on a flat base was an alternative *c* 1700–40, as was the scallop shell, made by the finest makers in the mid 18th century; superlatively fluted and pierced towards the edge, they were set on intricate cast feet, often dolphins or other marine creatures, and had a rising scroll handle formed as a marine or demi female figure. Baskets were made with the use of machine-made parts from *c* 1760, with geometric piercing and wirework, but with good cast mounts and piercing to *c* 1780. Oval, on a flat solid base, they were still decoratively varied with similar solid engraved forms *c* 1800. They are set on a pedestal base from *c* 1810 and are very varied, restrained and pretty to 1850, sometimes with radiating lobes, particularly on the Continent.

A silver gilt tea service with enameled decoration, by A. Greyton, Paris, 1862.

Bottom R: A coffee pot, creamer and sugar basin, silver inlaid with various metals, by Tiffany & Co., New York, 1878–80.

Neo-classical basket with geometric piercing by J. Hoyland & Co Sheffield, 1777.

THE TEA TABLE

TOASTING FORK

A long-handled fork for making toast by the open fire. Known from *c* 1550 (but probably earlier) when two-pronged and beautifully engraved, continuing to the present century. They may be up to 112mm (45in) long and are sometimes telescopic.

TOAST RACK

A tray with wire loops for holding toast. During the 18th century they were set on feet, with a ring handle, a frame replacing the tray from *c* 1800; made prolifically in surprising variety, frequently in Sheffield plate.

BANNOCK RACK

A triple-row rack for holding Scottish drop scones, known as bannocks, made during the 18th century.

Woven silver basket, London, 1786.

Large toast rack by Richard Whitford, Dublin, 1802; Gothic style, 1913, and a crown shape made as a commemorative piece for the coronation of Edward VIII in 1936, which never took place; both Birmingham.

Pierced basket in rococo style by Cornelius de Haan, The Hague, 1977.

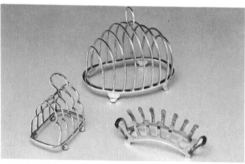

FLATWARE

Spoons dominate this subject, for the type of handle and decoration found on forks, ladles or other such articles, was that in vogue for spoons, the greatest single collector's subject. Spoons were important from very early times when each man carried his own. In Europe they were made both by the finest specialists and by the least proficient provincial smiths. They are collected for rare and interesting marks; for antiquity or historical interest; for quality of workmanship or for a combination of all such points, possible because some of the finest early spoons were provincially made.

EARLY SPOONS

The early English hand-forged spoon had a cast finial (styles summarized below), a flattened hexagonal stem and a fig-shaped bowl, the depth of which, *c* 1450, resembled a crescent moon when viewed sideways, with sharply sloping shoulders, becoming both rounder and flatter with time. Spoons of very fine quality were produced in the 16th century, their gilded finials joined to the stem by a V joint in London or by lapping

L to R: Rare early silver spoon, probably British, Roman period; Late 13th to early 14th century acorn knop spoon; Apostle spoon, possibly St Bartholomew 1490; Silver gilt seal top spoon, 1562; Buddha-knopped spoon, English west country 1630; Seal top spoon by Arthur Hazlewood, Norwich, 1638.

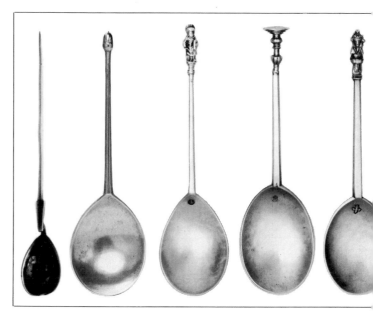

in the provinces; exceptions to such rules were the slip top spoon, *c* 1500–1650 (American 1670), which had the stem cut at an acute angle from the back down to the front; the stump top of the 17th century, its stem octagonal and molded into a pyramid (a European spoon, comparatively rare in England) and the Puritan, introduced from France via Scotland *c* 1630–70, presaging the flat spoon, its plank-like stem cut off at right angles and usually notched, the bowl becoming oval.

Finials were a frequent subject for forgery, faked casts of popular spoons, such as Apostles, either being added to broken-off stems or used instead of less desirable finials. Nevertheless, a single mold for a cast finial may be used repeatedly for a hundred years, losing sharpness but remaining genuine. Stem and bowl were made in one piece in England and America (except New York where Dutch influenced) but separately on the Continent, where early survivors tend to come mostly from Germany or Scandinavia.

Italian 16th-century knife fork and spoon sets were richly varied in renaissance style, the handles of knives frequently cast as human figures; Belgian combination folding spoons and forks often had a Virgin and Child finial and three-pronged forks were decorated in renaissance and transitional style. The cherub finial with a fig-shaped bowl and thin, tapering stem was originally a Norwegian speciality, *c* 1500–1635 (revived in early-18th-century Germany), their stems, like those of other continental spoons either twisted, twig-like or with other variations (*excluding* the English hexagonal type). Fig-shaped bowls were also common on the continent and usually engraved, frequently with flowers. Crown and berry tops were typical of Scandinavia (although also found in Germany), where early spoons tended to be very short.

Spoons depicting Biblical, classical, historical or romantic heroes, known as *Worthy Spoons*, were made in the 16th and 17th centuries, the personalities shown changing with popular fashion. One surviving set of these personifies the spoon-maker's art, with hexagonal stems, fig-shaped bowls with good thick edges and superlative figural finials.

Apostle Spoons *c* 1450–1650 were made singly, as a set of the four Evangelists or, ideally, as full sets comprising the Master and the twelve Apostles, each with his own symbol in his right hand, a book in his left.

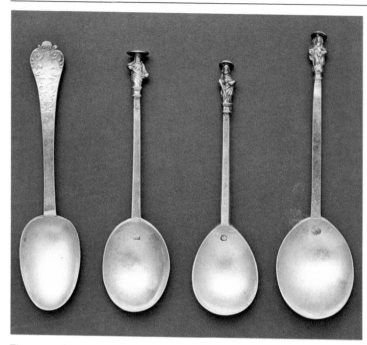

They were the most popular of early spoon finials and survive in surprising quantity.

L. to R. Trifid spoon, 1706; three Apostle spoons, 1594; St Matthew, probably Exeter, c 1650; Taunton 1660.

Finials of early spoons

Acorn (c 1300–1550). Both the Acorn and the *Diamond Point* are molded from the stem itself, unlike other finials which are soldered on separately. Thin stems, pear shaped bowls.

Wrythen (c 1350–1550). A spirally fluted finial.

Baluster (1350–1625). A flat round platform on a molded plinth, surmounted by a turned knop; of northern Dutch origin.

Maidenhead (15th century–1625). The head and bust of a young woman on a molded plinth, often so worn as to appear as a rounded knop.

Lion Sejant. An English speciality (15th century to c 1600 London, early 17th century in the provinces.) A seated heraldic lion on a plinth.

Moor's Head (to the 16th century). A small spoon

Dog-nosed tablespoon with rat-tail bowl by Henry Greene, 1701.

with a head usually too worn to define, possibly an infant Christ, later a Moor.

Berry (early 15th century, continuing on Continent). Berry-shaped finial common in Germany and Holland.

Owl (or squirrel or other small creature). Rare but formed from a family crest at any time; also a favorite alternative to hoof or caryatid in Holland.

Hoof. Swiss and Italian hoof spoons had a leaf-shaped bowl and a bone-like stem ending in a hoof. A very few such spoons were made in England between about 1550–1650. Similar spoons were made in Holland with an oval bowl, a few being made in this form in America.

Seal Top (late 16th century–mid 17th). The most prolifically surviving early spoon; a flat seal on a baluster, growing longer with time and dateable by exact form.

Disc End. Spoons with a circular flat disk were made in Scandinavia in the 16th century and in Scotland from c 1580–1660. During the mid-17th century they were also made in York, England, all for one family. Largely used as memorial spoons, a custom that continued in Dutch parts of US until mid 19th century.

Buddha. Early 15th-century spoons with a figure peculiar to Devonshire, England, probably brought from the east by sailors returning to Barnstaple, but possibly from Europe. Also known as Krishna or Vishnu knopped spoons for the knop figure has never been positively identified.

FLAT SPOONS AND FORKS

Stems were hammered flat from about 1660 (a little earlier in France), causing the notched end of the Puritan spoon to widen out to "trifid" shape. To strengthen this thinner silver an elongated "rat tail" ran down the back of the egg-shaped bowl from the base of the stem, and was sometimes surrounded by a lacy

A pair of three-tine forks showing back and front, by Mungo Yorstoun, Edinburgh, 1719.

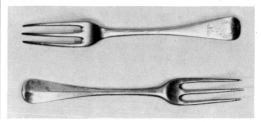

FLATWARE

pattern, decoration that may also be found on the front of the stem. The mid-century "picture back" provided a very interesting alternative to this lacy decoration for, although the picture was often political in subject, it could be very varied. A single "drop" gradually replaced the rat rail, starting in about 1700 in France, although the change was not complete until c 1730 elsewhere, by which time the overlapping double drop was also in use as an alternative.

Forks, long used in Italy and France, became general in the trifid period and had three prongs. Spoon shapes continued to evolve, the dog nose with its wavy end growing from the trifid before rounding off to become Hanoverian (c 1710–70) which was popular throughout Europe, the end turning upwards to meet the narrow ridge running up the front; this upward turn becomes less marked c 1760, when in the Old English pattern it turns down (on spoons but not on forks), the ridge also transferring to the back by 1770. This and the self-explanatory "Fiddle" pattern (c 1780 in France spreading elsewhere c 1790) and the "hourglass"

Knives and forks of various dates.

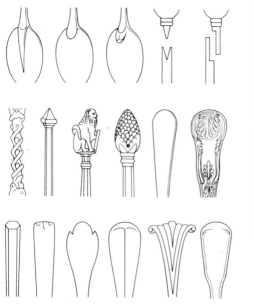

Spoon forms. *L to R, top row:* joints – rat tail, single drop, double drop, V-joint and lap joint. *2nd row:* 17th-century twisted Dutch stem; diamond point tip, c 1300–1500; lion finial, c 1400–1600; berry, from 15th century; old English; King's pattern, *3rd row:* slip top, c 1500–1650; puritan c 1630–70; trifid, c 1660–1700; Hanover, Onslow, fiddle.

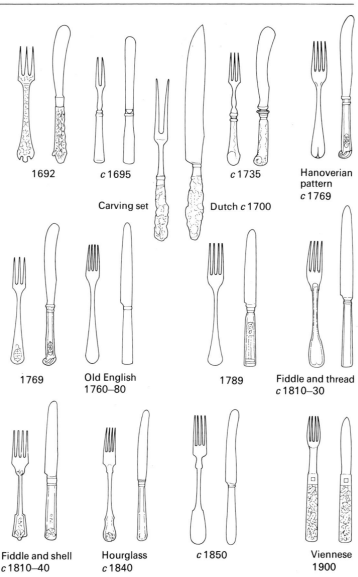

1692

c 1695

Carving set

c 1735

Dutch c 1700

Hanoverian
pattern
c 1769

1769

Old English
1760–80

1789

Fiddle and thread
c 1810–30

Fiddle and shell
c 1810–40

Hourglass
c 1840

c 1850

Viennese
1900

FLATWARE

which evolved from it are the basis on which most patterns are based thereafter. Variations on these general shapes are largely regional, such as the squared-off "coffin" end in Boston, or the thin Scottish and Irish spoons with their tapered stems and elongated bowls. Holland and Scandinavia continued with figural finials and varied stems as before, while "novelty" spoons, conforming to no generalizations, did occasionally appear at any time.

KNIVES

Originally carried personally, like the spoon; with steel blades, handles sometimes all silver or with decorated silver end caps and collars (ferrules) between the blade and handle of other materials. Pistol-shaped handles from c1700, then varied but increasingly following spoon styles. Folding pen or fruit knives from mid 18th century, a Sheffield speciality.

Complete services of flatware, with all sizes of spoons, forks and knives in the same style, were made for each other from c1790, usually excluding those for fish and fruit, but sometimes (particularly in France), including other table items such as salts.

Fruit or berry spoons, their handles marked for various dates, with Exeter and Birmingham marks, but their bowls added later, visible in a joint.

SPECIAL PURPOSE SPOONS AND OTHER OBJECTS

Sucket Forks. A combination two-tine fork and rat tail spoon joined by a straight section, used for sweetmeats etc *c* 1660. Less rare in America than in England.

Salt Spoons. Shovel shaped to *c*1740, then in enormous variety (including shovel), the bowl deep and round, often flared or fluted; handles in period styles or at the maker's whim; a good subject for the small collector.

Sugar Spoons. Long-handled, broad-bladed spoons, sometimes with a hooked top for hanging on to vase-shaped caddies. Now popular as jam spoons.

Fruit Service. Small gilt knives and forks rarely incorporated in a full service; handles of mother of pearl, agate or jasper with decorated silver ferrules and caps.

Berry or Fruit Spoons (19th century). Gilded rounded bowls embossed with grapes and vine leaves, the stems cast with vine motifs. Berry spoons are very frequently faked.

Caddy Spoons. See *Small Collectables*.

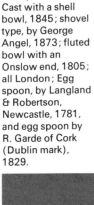

Salt spoons, *L to R*. Cast with a shell bowl, 1845; shovel type, by George Angel, 1873; fluted bowl with an Onslow end, 1805; all London; Egg spoon, by Langland & Robertson, Newcastle, 1781, and egg spoon by R. Garde of Cork (Dublin mark), 1829.

FLATWARE

Egg Spoons. Small spoons with a gilded bowl; from late 18th century.

Tubular-Handled Spoons (c1690–1710). A long tapering tubular handle with a baluster or ring finial, joined to a deep oblong rat tail bowl by a short straight section. Sometimes called "basting" spoons, they are invariably of superb quality, inconsistent with kitchen use; probably serving spoons. Made in England and popular in Ireland.

Hash Spoons (early 18th century). Serving spoons with extra long bowls, popular in Scotland and Ireland.

Marrow Spoons (pre 17th century). Rat-tail spoons, their handles formed as a scoop; these preceded the marrow scoop (although both made into the 19th century), with its long channel of different widths at either end.

Stuffing Spoons. Long slender table spoons, the stem very narrow centrally.

Gravy Spoons. Spoons with a fluted, elongated bowl, pierced in the folds, 300mm(12in) or longer, c1750. From c1800 onwards Irish fiddle pattern spoons were made with a central ridge for skimming gravy or other fluids.

Olive Spoons. Popular in France and other olive-growing countries, these spoons had a beautifully pierced bowl and narrow pointed end. Rare in England.

Mote Spoons. Similar to olive spoons but with a shorter stem, used for removing floating matter from liquids.

Infusor Spoons. 19th century spoons with a covered perforated bowl, sometimes in ball shape, in which tea was placed for infusing a single cup. Handles and bowls varied (often in inferior metal); amusing and inexpensive; all countries.

Modern Commemorative Spoons. Just one section of hundreds of thousands of today's spoon variations. Made everywhere, particularly in the US, they illustrate events, people and places of interest in the widest context, from the Christmas story and fairy tales to the happenings of last month. Cast, embossed, pierced, engraved or enameled, the event is recalled in the finial (particularly involving a personality); on the stem or bowl, frequently all three, the bowl usually in scenic form.

Butter Knives. 19th century. Knives with shaped, broad blades, charmingly engraved; green ivory or silver handles in period.

R: Straining spoons, half-pierced by Timothy Skottowe, Norwich 1638, fully-pierced by WC, London, 1641.

Far R: Pierced mote spoons; rare picture back, engraved on back of bowl, c1750 by Elizabeth Jackson; small rat-tail spoon, pierced only with plain holes, c1700 and a miniature by Thomas Dexsey, 1755; all London.

Marrow scoop by Richard Pargeter, 1738 and a marrow spoon with scoop handle by William Scarlett, 1720; both London.

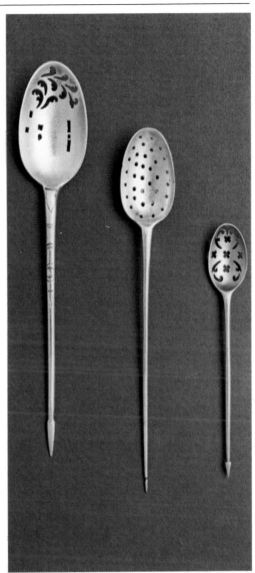

FLATWARE

Fish Slices. Flat, shaped, broad-bladed implements for serving fish, from *c* 1750; beautifully pierced and sometimes engraved, often with marine motifs. Silver handles in period style.

Pastry Slices. Basically similar to a fish slice; prevalent in Europe.

Cheese Scoops. Late 18th and 19th century long-handled shovels with a wide, shallow scoop for digging out cheese. In Scandinavia, where thin slices were preferred, a flat implement with a projecting blade to draw across the surface.

Salad Service. Not made purposefully before the 19th century and a popular subject for forgery. These consist of a spoon with a deep circular bowl (often modern and added to a well marked period handle), and a similar fork (its tines are often cut from a gravy ladle).

Ladles. Elegant long ladles for soup, from 1760, had deep, often fluted bowls, their Old English stems arched back and decorated in bright-cut. Sauce ladles considerably smaller and more sturdy.

Sugar Sifters. Pierced sauce ladles, usually geometric from *c* 1700.

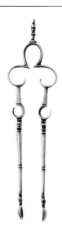

FLATWARE

Early sugar tongs in fire tong style, c1710.

Below L: Fish slice and fork, c1900.

Bow type sugar tongs with shell grips by Samuel Godbehere and Edward Wigan, 1794; Harlequin nippers, 1874, and scissor type nippers by John Lias, c1800.

Sugar Nippers and Tongs. Modeled on fire tongs c1685, becoming scissor-like 1725–60, with shell grips and a wide variety of stems; those formed as a stork, hinged through the eye and often concealing a baby, are rare, but were widely copied in the 19th century when the baby was considerably shorter. Cast tongs, c1770 and the bow type, in a single strip of silver (1780–1820), were made in all spoon styles with long pointed grips, inexpensive and varied.

Skimmers. A flat, half-perforated blade was used by confectioners for boiling sugar, c1735–50. Similar pierced spoons with long thin handles were used for removing foreign bodies from holy wine, very early or, c1690–1750, for removing lumps in the gravy.

Grape Scissors. Made as scissors with plain ring handles from c1800, the arms heavily decorated later, usually with vinery, when more like garden secateurs.

Asparagus Tongs. Surviving from c1745, narrow scissor-like tongs, ridged inside, becoming wider and sometimes pierced.

Nutcrackers. Usually silver plated steel, tong-shaped silver crackers, c1800, having proved impracticable.

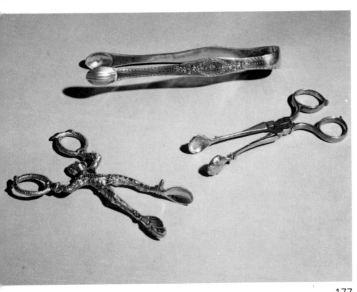

LIGHTING

Candleholders, Lamps and their Accessories

Although candlesticks were used in the home from early times, survivors pre 1660 are rare everywhere. However, existing examples show that they were quite magnificent in Italy, with figures in relief, or statuettes as a part of the stem. Those with a pricket to hold the candle would have been for church use. Between 1660–1685 candlesticks were only 125–150mm (5–6in) high and hand raised from sheet silver; they have a fluted Doric or clustered column stem mounted on a plinth set on a broad square or polygonal stepped base, a disc of similar shape above the socket as a drip pan, and another dividing the column from the plinth. These became a little more decorative towards the end of the period, but if elaborate with rich embossing or engraving they are Dutch inspired, as are all with clustered columns. The earliest candlesticks known in America (where always rare) were made in New York in this style (a very few on a flat base come from Boston), but the majority are from Scandinavia and Holland with some magnificent French examples; in Germany spiral stems on a high rounded base were considerably embossed, with wide drip pans, repeated below the stem. The form might be similar or baluster between 1685–1700, gadrooned on all the edges, the drip pan disappearing.

18th century

Candlesticks were first cast in France *c* 1690, the technique being rapidly adopted everywhere, and thereafter all were cast until *c* 1760, height gradually increasing throughout. France also originated the simple "Queen Anne" style in about 1680 and was copied enthusiastically everywhere (in Britannia standard silver in England *c* 1700–20). Bases in this style were circular, hexagonal or octagonal with a baluster stem reflecting the form of the base, the reel-shaped socket above a narrow neck sometimes doing so. The base was still wide in comparison with height and the only decoration was engraved armorials or a crest. During the second decade of this period in England the base, stem and socket might be facetted with diamond or other cuts and from 1720–30 a sunken depression around the centre of the base, which might be incurved or with cut corners, added to the surprising variety of silver that is dependent entirely

Candlesticks. *L* to *R*,
top row : Pricket candlesticks for church use, *c* 1650; clustered column, *c* 1660–85; octagonal sunk base baluster, *c* 1685–1700; Doric column, *c* 1660–85.
2nd row : Octagonal baluster, *c* 1700–10, considerably decorated in France; figural, *c* 1740; Corinthian column, 1760–70; early neo-classical, 1760–75.
3rd row : Baluster, *c* 1760–75; Dutch rococo, 1760; German column, 1790–1810; German fluted, 1795–1805.
4th row : Regency, 1800–20; a jumble of style, *c* 1825; heavily Victorian and ornate, *c* 1840–75; German, 1845.

LIGHTING

on line and quality. Such shapes were universal, but before 1720 the French were using considerable decoration on them, with flutes and lobes on all edges, medallions, foliage etc on the stem and flat chasing with a matted background around the base. Spanish candlesticks were similar, but those from Italy and Ireland (smaller) were plain, and from other countries only scantly decorated. From *c*1730 the candlestick begins to heighten and the weight of metal to decrease, pronounced shoulders and knops gradually taking on more ornament in the French style, becoming asymmetrical by 1740, with shells and other rococo motifs finally affecting every part of the stick, swirling, fluting and scrolling in exuberant, but rarely ornate, form. At the same time some examples were made in a more restrained manner, or even totally plain form. Shapes also varied within basically baluster formula, with detachable nozzles from 1740, the base circular but enormously varied and sometimes raised on scrolls, dolphins or something similar. French goldsmiths were even more varied and imaginative, particularly in border design, human bodies sometimes draping themselves most realistically around the scrolling stem. British goldsmiths also made figural candlesticks,

L : Early silver gilt filigree bougee box Scottish, *c* 1690; a continental waxjac and a bougee box with hinged lid by Benjamin Mordeca London, 1788.

A pair of cluster column candlesticks in William and Mary style, 1702.

reviving styles from the late 17th century; these took several forms, often orientally inspired, but include the rare Blackamoor, featuring a kneeling African figure on a triangular footed base, holding a wide drip pan and socket above his head, about 150mm (6in) high, and the caryatid, a form copied from the Dutch, in which the figure rises from a domed rococo base, holding the socket on her head with one hand; also made in Sheffield plate from c 1755.

The Germans, normally unhappy in rococo, were at their best in the style with candlesticks, if somewhat over ornate. Stems rose from a very high domed base, often shaped, copied in the Baltic states, Scandinavia (decorated with swirling fluting) and Holland where, although rare, they were distinguishable by applied spiral foliage. Scottish work, now generally similar to the English, used extra large sockets on candlesticks.

Tall Corinthian columns (1760–70) heralded the classic revival (c 1760–1800); 250 or 275mm (10 or 11in) high on a square base, itself used in transition with a baluster stem, these were decorated with gadroons or occasionally other neoclassical ornament, and were cast or die-stamped (not fully efficient as a technique before c 1770), the nozzle and socket still

andlesticks, *L to* Fluted neo-assic by Charles-ouis-Auguste oriman, (Master aris 1775), 1782; exican 1760; ctagonal by ancis Turner, 716; taperstick see p. 184), James ird 1720; and avid Willaume, 696.

LIGHTING

cast. At the same time a cast, tapering, baluster stem with a bell socket on a circular base was popular, heavily fluted and decorated with acanthus leaves and other classical motifs. Another early type was a concave column rising from a square base, its four-sided shoulders decorated with ram's heads, festoons etc on the base and an urn- or reel-shaped socket. These were frequently die-stamped in Sheffield, a speciality of the city whether in silver or fused plate, where dies were very sharp, permutations of ornament, column, base and socket becoming almost endless, each part taking any simple but elegant shape, fluted or spiral, sometimes polygonal, with all forms of light neoclassical decoration, or in former styles. Whether cast in London, die stamped and loaded in Sheffield (easily damaged) or made by either method anywhere else in the world, candlesticks of the period are tall (250–325mm/10–13in high) elegant, and in the same wide range, with fluting and decoration more closely grouped in France, classicism more truly adhered to in Italy.

After 1800

Decoration became much heavier after 1800 when, although previous shapes were still used, they were

A pair of 3-light candelabras in new classic style, by Paul Schofield, London, 1784.

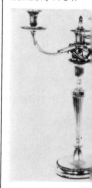

Rich figural 3-light candelabra by Frederick Kandler, London, 1747.

Two branched candelabra (see p. 184), by James Shruder, London, 1742.

182

Two branched candelabra, swirling in simple rococo style, by J. Bückenauer, Augsburg, 1743–7.

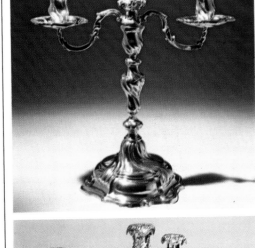

A pair of 4-light candelabras their triangular plinths set on lion supports, c 1810 by Matthew Boulton, Birmingham, in the style of Paul Storr.

183

LIGHTING

more often tapering, either in the round or square form, with the Roman and Egyptian form of classical decoration, sometimes beautifully cast. Purely classical or exotic, figural candlesticks, revived yet again, at their most popular in the 1820s. Candelabra became increasingly popular, the single holder losing importance until oil lamps virtually took over c1840. These trends were general except in France, where design is plainer from 1810.

TAPERSTICKS

Miniature replicas of candlesticks for holding tapers used for sealing letters c1685–1775, when coiled tapers virtually replaced them. Rarely in pairs or in exotic form except for the figural Harlequins (usually by John or William Cafe, c1740–60) featuring a figure in harlequin costume holding aloft a petaled drip pan below a bell-shaped socket; sometimes one hand on hip, when the drip pan is balanced on the head, steadied by the other hand.

WAX JACKS

Holders for a coil of waxed tapers (from c1680) when the taper was coiled around a vertical stem on a stand, the burning end held above in a vice of scissor-like form. They became more common c1775, when the taper was coiled within a tiny cylinder, often found in a writing case.

CANDELABRA

Candlesticks with branched arms, so increasing the lighting potential, were made from c1660, their popularity increasing during the 18th and 19th centuries until the coming of gas light c1840. Until 1770 two-light branches were most usual, a flame, urn or other finial surmounting a sleeve that fitted into the candle holder; thereafter two, three or more, increasing to the massive multi-light statuesque examples of the 19th century, up to 1500mm(5ft) high.

Branches were frequently made of Sheffield plate set on a silver stem and occasionally complete candelabra were made in Sheffield plate *en suite* with a set of candlesticks in silver; branches frequently made later to fit old silver candlesticks; national styles in period throughout.

DWARF CANDLESTICKS

For desk use 1680–1770, or on a pivoted bracket of a piano, with a wide base and a minimal stem, continuing through Victorian times, but usually of brass, or occasionally Sheffield plate.

Silver lamp in the form of a cupid by Giovacidino Belli, Rome, 1805.

184

CHAMBERSTICKS

Late 17th–mid 19th century saucer candleholders for carrying up to bed, with a straight hollow handle to *c*1700, gradually becoming shorter until replaced by a scrolled ring handle *c*1745. Ideally complete (when value is greatly enhanced) with a conical extinguisher, held on a lug on the saucer and scissor-like snuffers (after 1735) held in a slot below the raised socket. Rarely decorated beyond armorials and sometimes a border in the 19th century.

LIBRARY LAMP

For reading by a constant adjustable light, increased by use of a reflector, which also shields the eyes. Made in the late 17th century in Italy, where it originated, and in Spain, and in most countries throughout the 18th century. Two or more candleholders on a saucer base (very like a chamberstick and sometimes also complete with snuffers and extinguisher) are moved up and down a vertical pole: decoration, if any, found on the shield.

TELESCOPIC CANDLESTICKS

Adjustable to varying heights, this 19th century Sheffield speciality was often made in plate.

SNUFFERS

Scissor-like objects with a small box near the end, into

amber
dlestick by Isaac
er, London,
17.

pair of chamber
dlesticks by
er & Co.,
nburgh, 1835.

LIGHTING

which the wick falls, used for trimming the wick of a candle, not for extinguishing it. Probably made before the 15th century to *c* 1825, when the wick became self-consuming. Fairly simple decoration includes armorials on the box; and varied edges; handles are occasionally scrolled or decorated during the rococo period and quite ornate in the 19th century. When they have been made for use with a tray there are three studs under the handles and point.

SNUFFER STAND

An upright stand for holding snuffers *c* 1680–1725 shaped to contain the box, the part of the stand which, together with the edges, is the most often decorated.

SNUFFER TRAYS

Trays on which snuffers could be laid when not in use co-existed with stands but continued on to *c* 1825. Waisted rectangular or oval trays with one handle centrally, on three bun feet. Edges are decorated in many ways, the center generally engraved with arms. After *c* 1770 galleried surrounds appeared, attractively pierced; boat shaped from *c* 1785.

ARGAND LAMPS

Wall-mounted lamps patented in 1784 by a Swiss doctor who had earlier invented the self-consuming candle wick. Frequently made in Sheffield plate, they have an urn-shaped oil container, sometimes octagonal, with a domed cover and projecting arm (or two) holding a tubular burner with a tall glass shade.

Snuffer stand and its snuffers by Francis Turner, London, 1738, and a silver gilt snuffer tray, by Christian Drentwett, Augsburg, *c* 1750

WALL SCONCES

Light reflectors surviving from c1660 and rare after 1725 although there are later replacements and copies. Made for great houses in large numbers, where most remain, they have a richly embossed wall plaque (even when made during the Queen Anne period) with a projecting arm or arms to hold candles (occasionally of human form on the continent) or in rare examples a projecting galleried disc. French survivors outnumber others.

'ine silver gilt wall
ɔnce, one of a
'r, Augsburg,
49–50.

THE BEDROOM

The adornment and beautifying of the person has always been time-consuming, ladies sitting hours before their mirrors for, although people might care little about washing, they cared a good deal about appearance. Some of the most famous toilet services are decorated with the cypher of royal mistresses known to history (such as the French made "Lennoxlove" set, commissioned for Frances Stuart). Although the majority of toilet items are now found separately they come from so many nations that the general appeal of beauty is quite obvious. Nor is this confined to the ladies.

TOILET SERVICES

Dressing table sets were made for the ladies of Europe's most wealthy families by the very finest makers — and those surviving complete are mostly to be found in great homes, sometimes arranged on the table they always adorned, or in museums. These sets consisted of up to 30 pieces and included everything necessary for the lady's toilette, such as brushes and combs, clothes brushes, mirrors, candlesticks, snuffer and tray, caskets, bowls, scent bottles or flasks (with stands for those in glass after 1760), tray, salvers, sometimes a glove tray and occasionally a ewer and basin and soap

A 32-piece silver gilt toilet service mostly in rococo style, made in Augsburg, *c* 175.

Key to the compl toilet service.
1. Mirror,
2. coffee pot,
3. teapot,
4. ewer and basir
5. pin cushion,
6. candlesticks,
7. chambersticks,
8. matching pots caskets in diminishing sizes
9. covered bowl its salver stand,
10. snuffer tray w snuffers,
11. clothesbrush,
12. small covered pot with lug handles,
13. pair of salvers
14. small footed with hinged lid,
15. dish or finger bowl,
16. whisk,
17. knife, fork and spoon,
18 teaspoons,
19. inkstand,
20. vase shaped t caddy.

188

THE BEDROOM

box – particularly in France where sets also included an écuelle. Surviving mainly from *c* 1660 (Germany in Queen Anne simplicity from the early 18th century), when both Louis XIV and Charles II showered their ladies with extravagant gifts, of a standard never surpassed. Decoration, always including armorials, was the finest each age could produce, strongly embossed pre 1700 but sometimes in flat-chased chinoiserie in England during the 1680's; after 1750 when dressing tables were made with compartments, they are more often silver-mounted than solid. A large proportion of toilet accessories made 1660–1750, now found singly, originally belonged to such sets.

MIRRORS

The most important toilet item (*c* 1660–1850) setting the standard, style and decoration of the whole service. Shapes varied but were crowned by a superlative frieze with armorials or a plaque in the centre (religious in Italy), the amount of decoration greatest on oblong mirrors. Hand mirrors were rarely included in the toilet service, but were known in antiquity, the reflector being of metal before *c* 1200. Popular in art nouveau but the 19th century generally was prolific in a multitude of repoussé or simple initialled styles.

Hand mirror in pierced silver on a red ground, *c* 1680

rror of 1888,
ndon.

low R : Mirror by
ward Wakelin,
ndon, 1752.

elow : Mirror from
oilet service by
omas Bolton,
ublin, 1693.

THE BEDROOM

CASKETS

Beautifully fitted silver jewel caskets were made in 16th-century Germany (mostly in other materials elsewhere, but sometimes silver-mounted) while the Dutch specialized in tiny wedding jewel caskets during the 17th century. Made as part of a toilet service from c1660 for holding ornamental combs etc, they are larger than other toilet items, rectangular, sometimes with cut corners and often on low feet; their hinged lids provided a wide surface on which goldsmiths rose to their heights (particularly in France) whatever the period. Often converted during the 19th century for use as inkstands or to hold writing paper or cigars.

TOILET BOWLS

Part of a toilet service, with lift-off lids, or made separately in a variety of shapes, square, round, oval polygonal or shaped, to hold salves, pastes and powders for the complexion, or for the silk patches, used with great variety and skill in the 17th century to decorate the face. Made prolifically from 1880 in cut glass with a decorative silver top (art nouveau popular), or in pressed glass with a plated lid, they are widely collected, but tricky as rarely marked except in Britain.

BRUSHES

When part of a service, these are flat like a gentleman's hair brush, the silver back *en suite* with the service, or with a conical silver handle (both also made separately). Silver-backed hairbrushes, engraved, engine-turned or embossed were popular in late 19th and early 20th centuries.

Octagonal brush with chinoiserie decoration, London, 1683.

Bottom R: A casket by Pierre Harache senior (the first Huguenot to be admitted to the Goldsmiths' Co., London in 1682), c1700.

Gadrooned oblong casket, its Britannia marks clearly shown, by John Boddington, London, 1701.

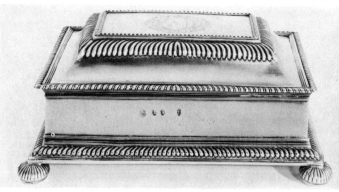

THE BEDROOM

SCENT BOTTLES

Although probably used earlier, scent bottles or flasks made entirely of silver are known from the 16th century, when they were a flat vase shape, with chain-secured stoppers, similar to a Pilgrim bottle. Made somewhat larger for 17th century toilet sets in square or pear shapes with a hook, ring or bun top, they were generally of heavy quality and decorated in period. Chain stoppers continued in use on the continent, even when cut glass with silver mounts became normal in the 18th century. Small bottles with tightly fitting silver stoppers for the handbag, slightly larger for the bedroom, were made in every shape in the 19th century, creating a very collectable subject.

Art deco hair brush, 1934; silver backed Birmingham, 1914, and a whisk, London, 1912.

Silver topped glass scent bottles, spiral 1889; man in the moon, Birmingham, 1896 and snake with garnet inset Birmingham, 1901.

A selection of Victorian silver-topped perfume bottles in colored glass.

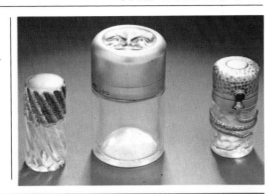

THE BEDROOM

GLOVE TRAY
More usual in the French 18th-century toilet service than elsewhere, similar to a footed oval salver.

COMBS
First known 3100 BC in ivory, topped with a hippopotamus; Scythian gold combs (8th–4th century BC) were unsurpassed for beauty. In the 17th century they were usually tortoise-shell, silver-mounted in dainty filigree, with hair slides and grips, sometimes in silver, dating from *c* 1650; long toothed crescent combs of great variety and delicacy, and two- or three-tined hair ornaments, occasionally made in silver, appear in the 18th century, particularly in Germany. Those made in quantity for practical use from *c* 1900 are straight with silver tops, and when designed for the pocket they slide into decorated silver cases.

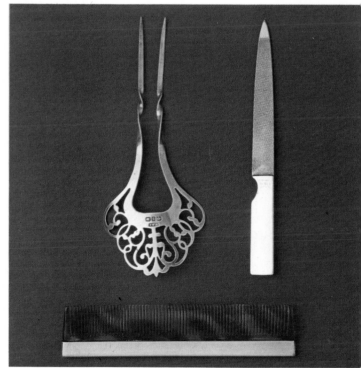

Nail file and comb, Tiffany & Co., New York, 1970; ornamental comb, Birmingham, 1899.

HAT PINS

These have a history similar to combs but they were made prolifically after 1900, with steel shafts and die-stamped silver terminals, sometimes commemorative or political, such as those featuring women's suffrage in England.

CURLING IRONS

Most popular when hair was waved in the 1900s and in the 19th century for curling hair, when smaller examples were for curling the gentleman's beard or moustache. Those in silver, with richly decorated handles, were held over a spirit burner on a similarly decorated stand.

DRESSING SETS FOR MEN

Silver-mounted mahogany cases were quite usual for men, particularly on their travels, containing toilet

Gentlemen's toilet set in blue-lined mahogany case, comprising ten cut-glass bottles with silver gilt mounts, a silver gilt beaker and a tray of accessories, English, 1824–7.

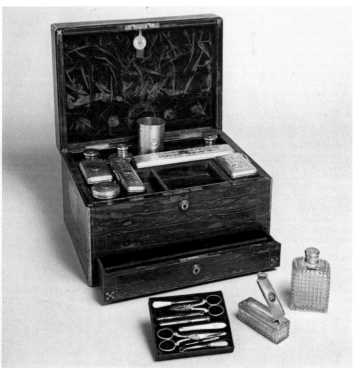

THE BEDROOM

essentials such as shaving kit, toothbrushes and a surprising number of pots for soap, salve and scent, all ingeniously packed.

SHAVING DISHES or BASINS

Very like an oval meat dish — from which they have occasionally been made — with a semi-circular section cut out from the rim (for holding against the neck). Known from early 16th century, they are essentially simple, in excellent quality, with armorials engraved on the rim and possibly a gadrooned border. In 18th-century Spain or Portugal a kidney-shaped dish was used, the crescent fluted out to a beautifully shaped rim; usually accompanied by a decorated, helmet-shaped jug.

SHAVING JUGS

Made *en suite* with their basins, but once separated they are rarely distinguishable from any other jug of their period, although essentially simple.

SHAVING POTS

Amongst the small containers in a fitted travelling case is one with a detachable handle, stand and spirit lamp, making a shave possible anywhere.

RAZORS AND RAZOR CASES

A case for razors belonging to the Barber-Surgeon's Company of London, *c* 1515, is cast with figures of saints and possibly indicates English standards at the time. During the 17th century, when a razor a day was the rule, they were silver-handled and kept in a case similar to those used for knives, often complete with scissors, strops and curling irons.

SOAP BOXES or SPONGE BOXES

Spherical containers, with a circular foot and a pierced lid, made in the 18th century, are for soap on the continent, the piercing often very fine in France, but usually for sponges in England, although sponges were themselves sometimes silver-backed, like a clothes brush.

EYEBATHS

Eye-shaped bowls, on comparatively high stems, with an oval, stand foot, were known in the 17th century but made in quantity from *c* 1800 onwards.

TOOTHBRUSH

A silver frame into which a succession of ivories set with bristles could be placed; the long decorated handles are often waisted. Mainly *c* 1750–1850.

TOOTHPICKS

Silver toothpicks were shaped for teeth at one end and

A Dutch 18th century toy warming pan, *c* 1720.

Silver shaving brush by Thomas Ellis, London, 1794.

Eyebath, Birmingham, 1925; Toothpaste tube winder, Tiffany, New York, 1970, and a shaving brush container, Walker & Hall, Sheffield, 1902.

THE BEDROOM

cupped for ears at the other; (17th and 18th centuries).

TOOTHPICK BOXES

Silver boxes with engraved lids hinged lengthwise; for carrying toothpicks in any material; mostly late 18th century.

TOOTH CLEANING BOX

A larger version of the toothpick box from c1775, containing toothbrushes; a box for tooth powder (itself double lidded, hinged centrally) and a tongue scraper from c1800 (a springy bow with a moulded section at either end).

WARMING PANS

Rare in silver; a flat covered bowl with a beautifully pierced top and a long wooden handle; filled with burning charcoal and placed in the bed; mostly 17th century. (Fire extinguishers were not made *en suite*!)

BUCKLES

Used for fastening knee breeches; shoes, sashes or cravats, curved, rectangular form, the silver rims taking a great variety of ornament. Ranging from about 37mm (1½in) to very large in France, c1750. High fashion in the late 18th century, when in England Birmingham workshops alone made 2½ millions annually, in US output was comparable. Another prolific period was in the late 19th century when they were made in art nouveau styles, a period when fine buckles were also made by American Indians. Small buckles were also used on garters. Almost all had steel pins, resulting in rust so that comparatively few survive, but they are collected avidly.

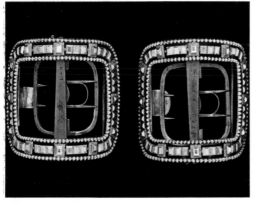

Pair of silver gilt and steel buckles, J. Jacobson, c1810.

BUTTONS

A very wide subject to which periodicals are devoted and on which books are written. Used prolifically in every country throughout history, at times of high fashion they were often converted from other objects, such as hat pin tops, brooches or coins. In the late 17th century Salzburg, like other mint towns, soldered shanks behind coins, sometimes obliterating their dates; toggle links were also used. In America, where the first settlers considered buttons a vanity, they were later made for trade with the Indians, often using coins. Other toggle-linked buttons were also used on clothing, the links themselves sometimes being very fine; Dutch examples, up to 68mm (2½in) across, were used for fastening baggy trousers. Mountain countries in particular have used buttons decoratively on national costume, the lacings of bodices strung between, the buttons themselves essentially decorative, in filigree etc. In India they formed part of the

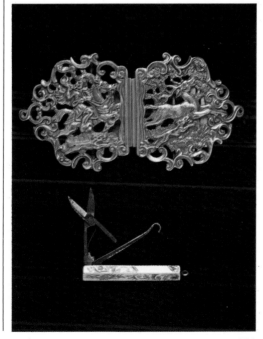

Silver gilt buckle and a button hook and scissors within a hooked container, American.

THE BEDROOM

trappings on elephants, hanging from a ring on top, heavy, magnificent and varied; In France they were used only for decoration in the 13th and 14th centuries, but importance grew during the 16th, so that between 1600 and 1700 thousands were employed in their manufacture (as in Birmingham, England, in the 18th and 19th centuries). Button styles are almost limitless, varying a little with current fashions: purely decorative, political, clubs, and sporting – with foxhunting a very popular subject for them in England and America (where it was introduced c1650). Made in every conceivable material, often silver-backed to hold the shank, they make an enormously varied collector's subject.

BUTTON HOOKS

Most necessary with stiff fabrics, shoes and gloves; surviving from 1800, particularly 1860–1925. Made with steel shafts and handles of many materials, particularly silver, they are decorated in a great number of ways, some carrying advertising slogans. A few fold, like a penknife, occasionally with several hooks of different sizes.

CLASPS

Not unlike a buckle but with a catching device replacing the pins, so allowing greater variety of decoration centrally.

Buttons: *Top row:* L to R, child, 1899; Elizabeth I coin made into a button c 1800; Celtic design, Iona, c 1900; Art nouveau 1904; *Third row:* Art nouveau, French, 1902; cow, Dutch 19th century; castle, Birmingham, 1910; Roman head, 1901; *Bottom row:* flower, 18th century; bow Mexican silver. Remainder probably 19th-century but could be as early as 17th-century.

Six Hunt buttons, John Sanders, London c 1790.

SOCIAL ARTICLES

Concerning objects used in public for pleasure, letter writing or sewing.

INKSTAND (STANDISH)

Surviving from *c*1630, when these containers for ink and its accessories were mostly in casket form, doubtlessly for the convenience of traveling scribes. Then came a footed, oblong tray, which varied little except in decoration from *c*1700–1825, and was fitted with sockets for holding the various containers necessary to letter writing. These consisted of an inkpot, which has a small receptacle for ink within another which is filled with shot for cleaning the quill nib, itself laid in a trough to the front when not in use; a pot for pounce (a special kind of sand) with a perforated lid for sprinkling on the absorbent paper before writing and also for drying the ink afterwards, and a wafer box necessary for sealing the letter. Ideally there is also a bell for calling a servant to deliver the letter and a taperstick for melting the wafer with which to seal it. Feet and rims were the main decorative features, varying according to period, rims being gadrooned; simple, molded or scroll and shell, or beaded — but only rarely of exotic rococo form.

Shapes were largely variations on the rectangle, although there were always exceptions, including a fine triangular tray on three lion couchant feet by John Coney of Boston, *c*1700. Pierced galleried sides appeared *c*1760 (with galleried sockets to hold silver mounted glass containers for traditional usage). The rectangular tray gradually became oval, and then boat-shaped with die-stamped parts. A circular or triangular tray was occasionally made from about 1800, holding a circular container, sometimes in the form of a globe on a stem, but by then the massive inkstand in very varied form was becoming popular. The earlier trays continued, but in heavier form, the Dutch retaining the gallery. A great number of inkstands in plain, tasteful form were made in Italy at all times, although a few exist in current styles.

PEN TRAY

From *c*1770 and very similar to the waisted, oblong snuffer tray.

SEALS

Surviving from the 12th century and made in great quantity, particularly in the 18th century, for impress-

Casket form of ink stand with two of its pots shown separately, by John Ruellem, *c*1670; an inkstand with a bell, Oporto, *c*1865 and a pen tray by Wilkinson & Co., Sheffield, 1830.

SOCIAL ARTICLES

ing upon wax the image of a distinctive device which has been engraved upon metal in reverse. They range from the Great Seals of royalty to the most ordinary family crest. Many provincial hall marks have taken the arms of the city concerned which may also be seen on their civic seal. Comparatively few seals survive, but those that do have often been made into signet rings.

PAPER KNIVES

Made in modern times with flat blade and silver handle, textured surfaces and interesting shapes.

BELLS

From the earliest celtic bell shrines to the present day, bells have been used in the Roman Catholic Mass, as a medieval ornament, as race prizes in 16th-century England and as a summons. Table bells, calling diners, are larger than the inkstand bell, but otherwise similar and of superb heavy quality, although rare in England where servants were generally present. They were very popular in US from c 1800, the handle taking many forms including cherubs, animals, pirhouetting ballet dancers or Chinamen, the ringer formed as a long dress, fruit etc, or in conventional shape.

PASTE POTS

Glue replaced seals for letters in the 19th century and was held in a pot with a twisted C scroll handle on an attractively varied saucer, a brush inside the lid.

Pounce pots, one as a watering can, London, 1882, and in purple glass, 1898, with two American letter openers, 1913.

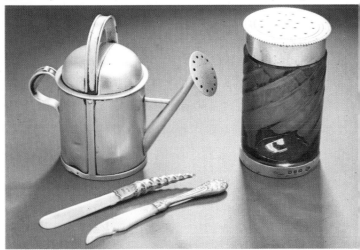

206

SOCIAL ARTICLES

INK ERASERS
Knives with a short shaped blade and die-stamped silver handle made in the 19th century for scratching out blots or, in the US from c 1890, a die-stamped silver mount gripping a hard eraser at one end, a brush at the other.

STAMP BOXES
Tiny die-stamped boxes with a slip-on cover and a ring on the top corner, for attaching to a chatelaine, 19th century.

PROPELLING PENCILS
In very varied forms since 1822, from the sedate gold cylinder to the most incongruous novelties (mostly US) such as a pig with lead emerging from its mouth when its tail is pulled.

PENCIL CASE
Mostly 19th century, made in silver in any long shape, such as a Corinthian column, a walking stick etc, or a decorated box, often inscribed for presentation.

PENKNIFE
Originally for sharpening quills, these folding knives are almost indistinguishable from Sheffield's fruit knives. Handles were of plain silver, mother of pearl or tortoise-shell etc, during the 18th century, but were later of decorated silver, at their most attractive in art nouveau.

Three table bells: *L,* by Simon Pantin, London, 1724; *R,* by P. B. van Linden, Amsterdam, 1769, with London, 1799, between.

207

SOCIAL ARTICLES

TOBACCO BOXES

Tobacco was brought to England from Virginia in about 1580 and its use for smoking or sniffing soon spread. Boxes for its use were made in England mainly from about 1660–1730; mostly oval with a detachable lid, they were usually engraved with armorials and possibly a motto around the sides. A few survive in silver-mounted tortoiseshell and other materials, but larger examples, set on imposing feet, are rare and mostly had a tobacco stopper attached to a chain. In Germany they were less simple and could be embossed with martial scenes, while in Holland they took several forms. Mostly made in Amsterdam during the mid 18th century, some had a hinged lid and might be engraved with an ambitious scene, but more often they appeared as a high, shaped box, octagonal or with canted corners, set on feet, sometimes with pierced scroll-work between them. Such boxes were lightly engraved and had a high domed lid, with a finial.

PIPES

Tobacco was mostly smoked in long clay "Churchwarden" pipes (sometimes cast in a silver mould), those in silver, c 1600–1850 being similar. Silver pipes were presented in peace to Indian tribes in the US, 1814. Hookah pipes and silver-mounted Meerschaum pipes, with a scraper attached to a chain, are also known.

Pipe case London, c 1670.

Bottom R:
Cigar cases, 1900, and with views of Warwick Castle, 1840 (both Birmingham) and, C, cigarette case, London, 1936.

Calendar pencil, 1937; bridge pencil, 1904; orange peeler and fruit knife, 1903, and a folding penknife, 1893, all Birmingham.

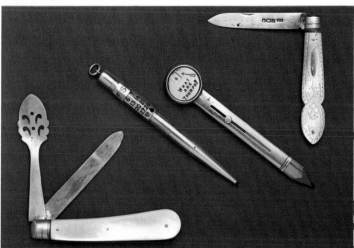

Pipe cases. Because early clay pipes were so easily broken, cases for their protection were used by the wealthy, sometimes richly decorated.

PIPE STOPPERS

Mostly made in base metals, ivory or wood, but occasionally silver, when of cast baluster form with a seal-like, flat base, used to press tobacco down in the pipe, some incorporating a scraper for cutting out the charred deposit inside. More imaginatively decorated on the continent, particularly Holland, and also popular in US (17th and 18th centuries).

CIGAR CASES

Made in Birmingham, England, from 1860, but never in the numbers or variety later seen with cigarette cases; both in hinged and flat carrying form.

CIGARETTE CASES AND BOXES

Cigarette boxes, in any material, shape and style, were made from *c* 1900, but novelties were always popular, incorporating an ingenious pop-up device or musical mechanism. Flat cigarette cases for pocket or handbag were equally varied but sometimes concealed erotic pictures.

SOCIAL ARTICLES

SNUFF BOXES

Boxes for powdered snuff were made from about 1725, the taker previously having used a pocket grater and a plug of tobacco. The habit was extremely popular and these small pocket boxes, with hinged lids for outdoor convenience, were made all over Europe and America, in every conceivable material. Sometimes very rich, beautiful and/or imaginative when made in England, Germany, Italy or Spain, the French stand alone for quality. From the richly chased gold box, set with brilliant jewels and enamels, to gold-mounted examples in many substances, such as mother-of-pearl, agate, ivory or lapis lazuli, they were decorated with enamel miniatures, painted subjects, or jewels, and were almost invariably magnificent. Rectangular silver boxes made in Birmingham, England, in the 19th century, a large number of them by Nathaniel Mills, are also characteristic. Sides may be engine-turned, reeded or embossed, but these boxes are known for their lids, representing sporting or mythological subjects, or public buildings collectively known as "Castle Tops." Occasionally engraved, these lids were mostly in strong relief, whether embossed or with a cast inset surrounded by embossing. Somewhat similar cases

Below L: Cigarette box with enamel inlays, Omar Ramsden, 1924.

Snuff rasp or grater, Phipps, Robinson & Phipps, London, 1813.

were made in Russia c1820, with nielloed pictorial tops, architectural, sporting or mythological, the silver lighter but shapes more varied.

SNUFF MULLS

Oval cylindrical silver-mounted snuff containers made in Scotland from the straight part of a horn (c1740), Edinburgh goldsmiths occasionally making them in fine quality silver with magnificent chasing. The Highland snuff mill, late 18th and early 19th centuries, a curled sheep's horn with silver mounts and hinge was usually engraved with thistle motifs (illus. p. 213).

SNUFF RASP

A large tubular grater for fining down a carotte of tobacco made before 1725, when tobacco was first sold ready ground.

R : A table lighter shaped as a Roman lamp, Birmingham, 1894.

Below : Snuff boxes: Cornucopia by Andreas Kierumgaas Saebye, Bergen, 1791 ; Shell by Matthew Linwood, Birmingham, 1803 ; engraved, Naples, *c* 1760 ; hare and hounds, London, 1819.

SOCIAL ARTICLES

CHESS SETS
The pieces used in this most ancient game have occasionally been cast in silver through the ages, usually in fancy forms, such as Shakespearean characters, but survive only from 1670.

CRIBBAGE BOARDS
Made in decorated silver, often with a drawer beneath for cards, c 1660–1900.

COUNTER BOXES
Wherever games of chance were played these boxes were made, usually in cylindrical form into which the coin-shaped counters fitted exactly. These were usually cast, occasionally beautifully engraved. English boxes were usually embossed on the lid with a medallion of the King's head, and mainly date from c 1660.

PERFUME or PASTILLE BURNERS
Of very ancient oriental origin and widely used when ventilation was poor and hygiene negligible, continuing well into the 19th century to provide a pleasant aroma. Made throughout Europe and surviving from the 17th century, these pierced bowls contained pastilles that emitted perfume when alight. Shape and decoration according to period, but very varied and of fine quality; popular in France where sometimes included in a toilet service.

THIMBLES
Surviving in silver mostly from the 16th century, but Roman thimbles are known. Made in every material

Charles I counter box with 35 counters, English, c 1630.

Perfume burner in neo-classical style by Boulton and Fothergill, Birmingham, 1777.

Snuff mull by W. & P. Kenyon, Edinburgh, 1793.

SOCIAL ARTICLES

from gold downwards, often as part of a chatelaine, or sewing set, they increase in numbers from the 18th century, when beautifully cast, but become thinner (and more easily damaged). They are very varied in the 19th century: sometimes topographical, moralising, advertising or commemorative, with plainer examples plentiful. Size, quality, theme and borders vary enormously, even within a given type. They were popular with American Indians and made in quantity for trade with them. In Scandinavia and Holland they are often decorated with enamels, the Dutch more pictorially; in France goldsmiths mixed metals and used precious stones. A subject of unlimited scope, inexpensive and small for display.

BODKINS

A long, blunt aid to threading ribbon or tape, attractively engraved; from c 1600, occasionally in gold.

PIN CUSHIONS

Padded cushions held by silver moldings of various designs, 17th century onwards; early ones are circular and often incorporated into the lid of a toilet pot. Frequently made as amusing novelties in the 19th century.

EMERY BAGS

Containers for an abrasive material used for cleaning rusty needles. Mostly 19th century, in strawberry or tomato form surmounted by silver foliage.

HEM GAUGE

A ruler with an embossed silver handle and a measuring clamp, used for regulating skirt lengths, 19th century.

SILK WINDERS

A small cross on which the needlewoman could wind her silks (not yet supplied on a reel); attractively varied and decorated, 19th century.

STILETTO

A long, adjustable, pointed instrument with a decorated handle; used for pushing out a hole without breaking the thread, for eyelet work such as Broderie Anglaise. Important in France and England to the early 20th century.

CROCHET HOOKS

The French art of crotchet was of ancient origin, requiring hooks of various sizes, unchanged through the centuries. Often of silver in the 19th century, but rarely decorated.

Two Elizabethan bodkins, English, c 1595.

adrooned
incushion on four
eet by Thomas
olton, Dublin,
693–5, and two
teel-lined silver
imbles, Chester,
905.

Below R:
Unmarked perfume
urner in the Dutch
tyle, *c* 1675.

DECORATIVE SILVER

Silver with little or no purpose other than to appeal to the eye.

TWO-HANDLED CUPS

The 17th century porringer, with its caryatid handles, became more upright and domed in the cover as it grew in height towards the end of the century, gradually developing into the solid ceremonial cup of the 18th century. This was set on a molded circular foot and was decorated around the lower body and on the high domed cover, with flutes or a calyx of acanthus or palm leaves before *c* 1690, then cut card work or applied strapwork (both French features like the harp handles, which in good quality cups were cast and hollow, and the molded rib often encircling the body). Continental goldsmiths soon lost interest but English cups were at their finest after 1720, Scotland a little later, both with some magnificent examples of exceptional quality, sometimes in gold, used as ceremonial loving cups or, increasingly throughout the century, as racing prizes. These were rare in America, but a bell-shaped cup was made there with strap handles and no cover; Irish work was also distinguished for lack of cover and for very heavy quality silver with little change until *c* 1790 (neoclassic) the stem only having grown meanwhile. In England the finest designers and goldsmiths rose to their heights with rococo cups using magnificent cast figural handles and embossed or applied cast decoration in great variety. The cup became taller and urn-like from *c* 1760 and was exceptionally well suited to the classic revival form, the best by Adam and other notable designers, frequently decorated with racing themes, horses and racing scenes embossed on applied plaques amongst a wealth of other classic motifs, and sometimes also on the finial. Early in the 19th century the cup lost its grace but increased in weight, with heavy decoration in Roman or Egyptian style, mostly applied ornament of very varied nature. These were almost always made for presentation, in recognition of achievement, or for sporting occasions, gradually growing in size until frequently several feet high, when they lost all form and importance. Their weight made such cups a favorite subject for duty dodgers who presented small discs for hallmarking before fitting them into the base of a cup.

VASES

Prolific in 16th-century France, and exuberant in 17th-

Top L : Early classic revival, the Richmond Race cup by Smith and Sharp London, 1764.

Top R : Two-handled cup and cover decorated with grapes and vines by John Swift, London, 1748.

Below L : A fluted cup and cover by Jonathan Porter, London, 1705.

Below R : Two-handled cup and cover by Paul de Lamerie, London, 1737.

DECORATIVE SILVER

century Naples, either complete with silver flowers, or in simple forms, vases (barely distinguishable from tall, tapering beakers) were produced for the church all over Europe, but did not reach England until introduced from Holland c 1660 as part of a garniture of chimney decoration consisting of tall beakers, 450mm (18in) or so high, or as bellied, narrow-necked Chinese ginger jars with small covers, set on a raised circular base (both nevertheless called "vases"), strongly embossed in the Dutch manner (a few in the 1680s in chinoiserie). Imitations of these were made in the 19th century, when large vases also appeared in the form of the Warwick vase, or of the two-handled presentation cups popular in classical Italy or in the French Empire style when they were frequently used as wine coolers. Classically ornamented and shaped narrow-necked vases for niche ornament were also popular throughout the century, but ordinary flower vases are very rare in silver. The American Tiffany and Company (using flower designs from c 1850) devised their own distinctive form of art nouveau by 1890, well suited to tall, very slim vases, often used as a silver overlay on

Vase in Chinese ginger-jar style.

Chinese-style beaker vase, made up to 580mm/23in high.

The Magnolia Vase in enamelled silver, designed by T. Curren for Tiffany & Co., 1893 glass or other materials. Taken up generally and made prolifically in Germany and Belgium.

PLAQUES

Ornamental plaques were made during the Middle Ages, wherever the guild system operated in Europe, particularly in Germany and countries influenced by her, such as Scandinavia and the Baltic states. Sometimes engraved when in silver but more often highly embossed, such plaques were made in all materials and mostly depicted mighty subjects — which could be scriptural, mythological or martial — usually glorifying one person or event. The boss of a mazer bowl or the centre of a great dish were made separately in similar manner as a part of the larger work but some purely decorative continental plaques were later used in the same way, when they were let into the base of large English pieces, such as rosewater bowls. During neoclassic times small oval plaques bearing horse racing scenes were made for application to two-handled cups, while small rectangular topographical or sporting plaques were made for the lids of 19th-century Birmingham boxes.

Embossed silver plaque, Dutch, 17th century.

DECORATIVE SILVER

GORGETS

Decorative breastplates, shaped like a child's bib, originated as armor but were soon worn as a badge of rank, engraved with regimental armorials. Indians were given similar objects when visiting American settlements in 1661, liked them and created the biggest demand, American and Canadian goldsmiths making them in quantity for Indian trade, and for presentation to Indian chiefs, suitably engraved in friendship and peace. A lesser number were made in Australia in the 1850s for loyal Aborigines. The majority of others to be found were made in England for ceremonial military occasions after 1750.

STATUETES AND FIGURES

Models of saints were made in quantity, particularly in Italy, Spain and Portugal from early times. Made as a part of a larger object since gothic times and now frequently found alone; small figures, animals or human, may have originated as finials on medieval cups or beakers (probable if under 75mm/3in), as figures decorating gothic or renaissance church silver, as figures on early tazze, salts particularly in Germany, or as stems of rococo candlesticks, or cups, salts, mustard pots etc, in period or as 19th-century revivals; when apparently incomplete statuettes may have been separated from a sculptural centerpiece. In England made as a separate entity only from *c* 1810, particularly as models of heroes such as Napoleon and Wellington,

Silver gilt statuette of angels, the bunc of grapes compose of seed pearls, Spanish, *c* 1600.

atuette by Omar
msden, London,
27. Although this
ece is very much
its period much
Ramsden's work
inspired by Celtic
d medieval art.
e often signed
eces as well as
plying his mark.

ontinental late
9th-century
gures in 18th-
entury costume.

DECORATIVE SILVER

in bust or full-length form, or on horseback, the fashion flourishing throughout the century and continuing as commemoratives until today, or as purely ornamental figures or groups in any contemporary or novelty style.

BOOK COVERS

Great Bibles, Gospels and Epistles are amongst the earliest of church treasures, bound originally wholly or partly in gold or silver, inset with jewels or enamels. Such manuscripts came from monasteries all over Europe and most have now lost their covers. The use of books spread more generally after the printing press appeared c 1450 and leather was used instead of silver (red velvet in England), tooled in fine designs in gold leaf, often with gold or silver corners and clasps; in dainty filigree or flower designs 17th century, particularly from Venice. Demand decreased sharply after 1700, but occasional silver covers for small books are still made.

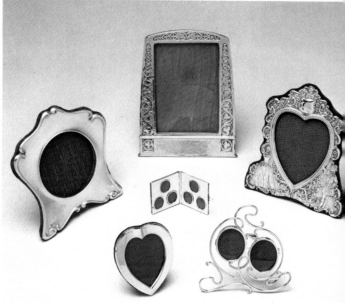

DECORATIVE SILVER

FRAMES

Picture frames of silver, similar to (and often converted from) mirrors, were not unusual during the 17th and 18th centuries. They were popular in France but most important in Italy, where large "cartagloria" frames were richly embossed and made for the church, often in triple form, to hold prayers. They were usually converted to mirrors when in private hands. Silver frames, particularly for photographs, were popular in the second half of the 19th century, richly embossed in any manner, and continued into the 20th century in art nouveau, art deco and other forms.

BRIDAL CROWN

Traditional in Norway where worn by brides since the middle ages and still used in the west with national costume. They are basically a ring with rising sections from which ornaments (often religious) dangle tinkling as the bride moves about.

SMALL COLLECTABLES

Small objects suitable for most collectors.

POMANDERS

Named from *Pomme Ambre*, the French ambergris apple, these perfume containers were the forerunners of the vinaigrette; and had themselves evolved from the 15th-century German musk ball, which in turn stemmed from pierced and bejewelled Roman beginnings. They were intended to combat infection or to offset the unpleasant qualities of stale air, and their ball-shaped bodies, with a ring finial, set on a raised circular foot (not unlike a Scottish bullet teapot) were divided internally into segments which opened out to take a sponge soaked in a pungent spiced vinegar or perfume. Although able to stand on a table they were usually worn suspended from the neck or chatelaine. Nearly always engraved, often with kings or other personages, the vast majority were made in Holland and Germany, and those made elsewhere, including England from *c*1580, were often engraved by immigrant Dutchmen, complicating identification. Rare after about 1630.

VINAIGRETTES

The use of air fresheners lessened, but never ceased, the vinaigrette evolving from the pomander, a few of box type being made throughout the 18th century. Nevertheless, the vast majority of surviving vinaigrettes were English, made in Birmingham *c*1800–75, as almost all those made before 1775, together with a few French and Dutch examples, have been lost. Those made in Norway, *c*1775–1800 survive in considerable quantity and variety, having been turned out from a mold. These tiny containers (from 12mm/½in mostly only up to 50mm/2in or so) come in many forms, fitted with a gilded inner grille, pierced to allow the aroma of spiced vinegar to circulate while holding the soaked sponge firmly in place, and with good double hinges (for lid and grille together), a perfect fit being

Three Birmingham Vinaigrettes, silver gilt by John Bettridge, 1830; Kenilworth by Nathaniel Mills, 1837 and one of 1863.

SMALL COLLECTABLES

imperative because of the somewhat caustic nature of the vinegar. The early rectangular form, with plain grilles, was replaced in Birmingham *c* 1790 by novelty shapes using lighter metal than the more stolid London boxes, and they continued until *c* 1875 (a few coming from London eventually), in very varied forms. Some were specialized, such as the snails of Matthew Linwood (the fifth of that name, working *c* 1790–1822, thereafter his son), but including such objects as flower sprays or baskets, crowns, books, birds, acorns, fish, lanterns, bellows, a strawberry and

A mixed collection of vinigrettes in great variety.

The grilles inside the vinaigrettes shown opposite.

SMALL COLLECTABLES

many more, all perfect in detail, complete with a fancy pierced grille (that may be a surprising and lovely picture in itself) and mostly well under 50mm (2in) in size. Commemoratives in various shapes were generally concerned with Nelson and Trafalgar (not Wellington or Waterloo) and date 1806–9. Cast top rectangular boxes (1830–65) are purely pictorial with good borders and fine filigree grilles, the famous "castle tops" appearing at the same time, usually fitted with repoussé lids, occasionally engraved. These were almost exclusive to Birmingham, where several excellent makers including Nathaniel Mills specialized in them. Their grilles were pierced into scrolling foliage and flower motifs, their lids recalling many of Britain's public buildings.

SMELLING SALTS CONTAINERS

Made from the late 18th century until about 1930, in flask form, sometimes in silver-topped glass, opening out to receive a standard vial of smelling salts. Nicely chased, they were purely functional and carried in the handbag.

CARD CASES

Although continental and American examples exist this is intrinsically another Birmingham speciality. Made from 1820 for the protection of visiting cards (which had been carried loose throughout the 18th century), they are rectangular, silver-gilt and were at first fitted with slip over covers. Rarely fully marked, they are inexpensive (except when made by Nathaniel Mills) and were decorated with dainty, simulated filigree patterns overall, interrupted by a cartouche placed centrally with initials. From c 1830 corners, previously sharp, were shaped, covers hinged at one narrow side, the filigree appearance, now used only above and below a central "castle top" panel, enhanced by superb pierced work, the same die sometimes used unpierced to totally different effect. Between 1830–40 each side showed a different scene, but one only from 1840, when the scrolling border outlined the building, sometimes engraved from c 1850. Castle tops continued to c 1880, when plain engine-turned designs (introduced from c 1850), art nouveau, revival styles or plain cases with initials, were more usual, straight edges less sharp than previously, having returned c 1900.

VESTA BOXES

When vesta matches were first made in 1833 they were

SMALL COLLECTABLES

Castle top card case by Frederick Marson, Birmingham, 1856, showing the Houses of Parliament.

Victorian vinaigrettes, mostly London made.

SMALL COLLECTABLES

highly combustible and were therefore carried in a box for safety, often a snuff box with a rasp added, on which to strike the match. Purpose-made boxes were introduced c1850 (although few survive) and these had gilded interiors to prevent spontaneous combustion, and a rasp incorporated into the design. These tiny boxes, rarely more than 50mm(2in), usually had rounded corners and were made in many countries, particularly England, where London predominated until 1888, when Birmingham became the main center of production. By this time they had become fanciful in shape with children, animals, musical instruments and other familiar objects very popular. They were often suspended from a watch chain, when a tiny ring will be seen, or carried in the pocket. They lose importance after 1900. Match box covers were also made in many countries, but largely in Birmingham from c1875, in many shapes and styles, (books, flasks, wheatsheaves etc;) they might also be plain, engine-turned or flat-chased. They are rarely marked although marks appear on the inner rim of English boxes; they are sometimes silver plated and usually inexpensive.

FREEDOM BOXES

The Freedom of the City was freqently bestowed on

R: Irish Freedom Box by James Keating, 1797.

Bottom R: Irish Freedom box by Richard Garde of Cork, Dublin, 1821, showing Cork city arms.

Below: Bulldog Vesta Box, Birmingham, 1906; inlaid with Connemara shamrocks, Dublin, 1913 and a repoussé Dutch scene, Dutch.

distinguished persons in 18th-century Ireland, the parchment enclosed in a circular box of gold or silver of about 63–88mm (2½–3½in). In very heavy quality metals such boxes, very occasionally chased, were normally engraved only with the arms of the city, Dublin, Cork (very high standards), Limerick and occasionally Youghal. Seal boxes, made for the safekeeping of important seals in England and Scotland, were similar in concept, but rather larger and more decorated during the 19th century.

MUSICAL BOXES

Almost invariably Swiss made, from the late 16th century, these boxes play tunes when the lid is opened, or a clockwork mechanism wound (a rotating cylinder plucks at tuned "teeth" inside). In gold, silver or other materials, often inset with enamels depicting mountain scenery. Any type of box was sent to Switzerland from abroad to be given the works, whether a casket, snuff box, or the tiniest vinaigrette. Novelty shapes particularly were always popular and musical movement might be placed in almost any form of container. Their mechanism may also be found set into objects such as a tankard, walking stick or the seat of a child's chair.

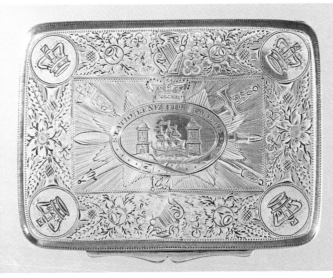

SMALL COLLECTABLES

OTHER BOXES

Authorities such as the Victoria and Albert Museum never differentiate between boxes, yet their original functions often differ and in many cases their form is recognizable. In others it is not. Unspecified boxes ranging from 25–100mm (1–4in) average, appear from virtually every country, from the late 17th century onwards. Decorated according to period and locality, with fine niello scenes from Russia and embossed battles from 17th-century Holland, etc. Many undoubted novelties, fulfilling a short-lived purpose; others described variously as cachou, pill, tinder, pounce, counter, coin boxes or something else, all lacking proof of identity.

NUTMEG GRATERS

Tiny containers c 1685–1835 (earlier as an anti-plague prophylactic), with lids above and below, intended for table use. Not liable for marking in England before c 1790, but roughly dateable by style and maker; cylindrical, their graters fitted immediately below the upper pull-off lid, the nut itself held at the lower end. From c 1685 they were very lightly decorated with scratch engraving; there was considerable overlapping of styles and dates, but roughly they followed in the

Three unspecified boxes, engraved oval by Edward Cornock, London, 1714; enameled, Christen Jensen, Copenhagen, c 1700 and Edward Jarrele, London, 1822.

Oblong nutmeg grater by Joseph Willmore, Birmingham, 1812.

order of heart shapes with hinged lids (1705–30), very small acorns (1730–55), and the egg shape from c1750, but most popular c1790 with bright-cut engraving. Throughout the period various other shapes might also appear, such as nuts, berries or shells, barrel shape (mostly c1750–1810), oval with pull-off lids (1770–85) or hydrants, in three pieces c1730–1810, all those of the late century at their most desirable with bright-cut engraving. Fully marked boxes, that were often engraved with inscriptions, appeared 1780–1820 (but mostly 1790–1810), together with large (up to 68mm/2½in) hinged, cylindrical graters, while fancy shapes continued. During the mid 19th century heavy, hinged boxes were used, often engine-turned, plain rectangular, or in fancy shapes. American graters in contemporary styles were made only up to 1720.

WINE LABELS (BOTTLE TICKETS)

A very large specialist subject in the British Isles where a wide variety of wines and spirits was put into unmarked bottles after 1660, as were lotions for gunshot wounds, sauces and other liquids, causing considerable confusion. A form of labelling was therefore necessary, and although any made on the

A set of wine labels complete with chains, the names cut out, by Rawlins and Dumner, 1842.

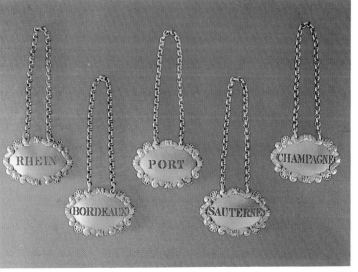

SMALL COLLECTABLES

continent were usually of other materials these were made in silver in Britain from *c* 1734, complete with two small eyelets or rings to hold the chain by which they were hung around the bottle. These early examples were escutcheon- (shield-) shaped and largely made by one maker, Sandilands Drinkwater. Crescent shapes followed, from *c* 1750, with reeded, feather wriggle or (after 1780) bright-cut edging, but well before 1800 (when the crescent had built up to many variations) other shapes were appearing and thereafter production increased to enormous proportions with labels made in every corner of England, Scotland and Ireland. The names of every known wine and spirit were engraved, chased or pierced upon them (and a great number that are less familiar such as shrub, arquebuscade, vidonia, uisgebetha or evocative eccentricities like "the Abbot's Bottle") and there are few shapes that were not used before a law made paper labelling compulsory in 1860, killing the craft. They were hand raised in London and Edinburgh, a family crest or coronet often incorporated in London, die-stamped in Birmingham (and largely elsewhere) in thinner silver, their superlative sharpness often lost after 1810 when a mold was sometimes used, standards falling generally after 1840. Scottish labels mostly remained plain and of good quality, styles elsewhere being too diverse to give more than some basic shapes and dates. They might be oblong or rectangular, sometimes polygonal or eye-shaped (largely Dublin), usually with reeded borders (octagonal always reeded) but also feather-edged, beaded or bright cut; with gadroons in Dublin. Width and decoration varied considerably and might include a domed or crested top, drapery or festoons, themselves liable to surround *any* shape in that period. Scrolled or openwork labels, sometimes quite exquisite, appeared from 1780, the period also of the star (rare), fouled anchor or the festooned urn; bright-cut adds value to any label. Heavy borders of bachanals, grapes, cupids, masks etc (cast in London), mostly date from 1820–50, while the matted vine leaf (*c* 1830) or escallop shell (*c* 1810) had the name pierced out or pierced and embossed on a superimposed ribbon. During this late period any previous style might be repeated and endless novelties, some of them quite magnificent, also appeared, the label formed as an initial dating from *c* 1835.

234

Preceding pages: A large selection of wine labels, showing the wide variety of borders or even the plainest labels; the lightness achieved by the neo-classical. Note particularly the Madiera, lower left on p. 232, and the sharp detail of even the heaviest, Champagne, on p. 233.

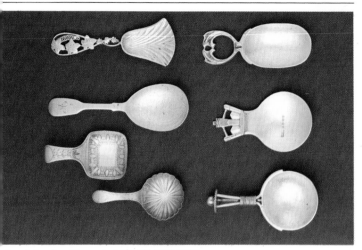

A variety of caddy spoons. *Top to bottom L :* Fluted bowl with grape-vine handle, Birmingham, 1886; fiddle-shape engraved bowl, London, 1849; square bowl, Birmingham, 1812; fluted bowl with flat cap handle, *c* 1777. *R :* A Jones, Birmingham, 1913; Jubilee design, R. A. Spoon, 1934; A. Jones, Birmingham, 1920.

CADDY SPOONS

A large seashell was packed with tea for export and this was originally used in England for scooping out the leaves. The first purpose-made caddy spoons, *c* 1770, were also shell-shaped (hallmarked only from 1781) and until *c* 1830 this always remained the most prolific basic style, although varied in many ways. The majority of shell spoons were hand-raised in London (until *c* 1830), their handles conforming to standard types : fiddle, Old English, Kings etc, with bright-cut engraving in period. The earliest caddy spoons were produced in Sheffield where the handle was a mere cuff, formed (as occasionally in Dublin), in one piece with the shell, while London handles were soldered on. Handraising was rare in Birmingham where die-stamping in thin metal reached the highest standards in plain or fancy forms; basic styles, the bowl round, square, oval or shovel, with standard handles were decorated on handles and/or bowls in every conceivable way, and continental examples, made in Holland and other countries, tended to copy these basic forms after 1800, mostly in fairly plain styles and usually in low grade silver, those of the US (very rare) being plain but in sterling standard. In England shapes continued to vary and the leaf, either in filigree (mostly by Samuel Pemberton of Birmingham) or with engraved veins, sometimes with coiled wire handles, was as varied as

235

SMALL COLLECTABLES

leaves themselves; die-stamped simulated filigree was frequent in the early 19th century. Samuel Pemberton used filigree insets in many ways but the majority of true filigree work 1790–1830 was Italian made in London. Fanciful shapes mostly originated in Birmingham (such as the jockey cap, a Joseph Taylor speciality, or the eagle's wing) but some rare spoons (the mussel shell, hand or some figurals) were cast in London. Caddy spoons were made throughout Britain until c 1860. Irish examples tend to be of larger size.

KNIFE RESTS

A small silver rod joining two cast supports, on which carving implements might be rested. Prolific in America, where they were also part of a place setting, for resting dinner knives. Made in many 19th-century forms; geometric, scrolling, animal, children etc.

NAPKIN RINGS

Purely functional from c 1760, but in a prolific variety of novelty forms in 19th-century Canada and America, particularly figural with delightful children playing, animals, etc.

Below L:
Corkscrew and holder, Rotterdam, c 1700.

Pair of Knife rests, London, 1839.

SMALL COLLECTABLES

Modern napkin ring, London.

Below R:
Corkscrew with mother-of-pearl handle and holder, Samuel Pemberton, Birmingham, *c* 1820.

CORKSCREWS

Have changed little since mid 18th century; basically of T-form, the cross handle of other materials, bone, ivory etc, the steel screw operating through a silver cylinder, sometimes open, often decorated. Many had a shaving type brush incorporated for cleaning the bottle top, and some had a knife for removing foil, or wire cutters for champagne bottles. The French travelling corkscrew folded the screw away in the handle.

CHATELAINES

A clip or brooch attached to the girdle or clothing, from which necessities were suspended in the days before pockets, normally carried by housewives from *c* 1740, for keys, penknives, notebooks, *étuis* (holding smaller necessities), pill boxes etc. They were made in silver or gold (rare) but more often in pinchbeck, ("poor man's gold," an alloy containing 5 parts copper to 2 of zinc, invented *c* 1730 by Christopher Pinchbeck). Something similar was used for suspending any collection of objects, carried by anyone, anywhere, from the beginning of time.

SMALL COLLECTABLES

ETUI
A case containing objects themselves too small for individual suspension from a chatelaine, such as thimbles, bodkins, pencils etc; originated in France c1750, where sometimes gold and bejeweled; more usual in silver, decorated in period, or pinchbeck. Cases for medical instruments, shaving equipment etc, were similar.

SPECTACLE FRAMES
A folding pair survives from c1635, complete with its beautifully engraved case, bearing armorials, but they are rare before c1760. Made in quantity everywhere but from 1800 in England (Birmingham), and America, where they were round or oval, frequently folding, with sides pierced for retaining ribbon, sometimes still complete with lens; bifocals from 1802; hinged for additional dark lens, 1824. An original case adds value.

BABY PACIFIERS (Rattles, teething sticks, and dummies)
The need of a baby to chew on something hard, to suck when sleepy and to make noise when happy, was catered for long years before Christ. Coral was believed to have great power and was used in nearly all teething sticks, rattles and dummies, frequently combined in one gold, silver or gilt mounted object known as a "coral." Continental examples, mainly Dutch, French and German, survive from the 17th century, but they were rare in England or America before c1750. During the 18th and 19th centuries cast silver decoration was considerable, the complete object (any part of it might be made separately) consisting of a curved coral

Engraved silver teether with whistle and coral, by Elizabeth Morley, London 1807.

Spectacle frames, c1820.

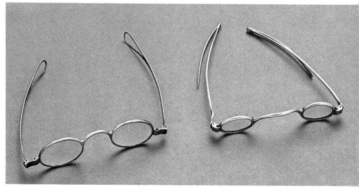

handle to hold or suck, a central knop hung with bells, to shake, ending in a whistle (a noisy dummy) and a silver ring for a retaining chain (even pre-Christian babies threw toys out). Later mother-of-pearl sometimes replaced coral, or bells were hung from an ivory teething ring.

SPURS

Ornamental or ceremonial spurs have long been made in silver or gold (a badge of rank), the oldest in England being part of the Coronation regalia. Made in quantity particularly in London, Birmingham and US, late 18th and 19th centuries; small, dainty and with revolving rowels, utterly unlike those made for cockfighting, which were rarely in silver.

BOOKMARKS

A late 19th-century development in the form of a thin slice of engraved divided silver, slipping over a page like a paper clip; a ribbon with silver attachments at either end, in any conceivable form, or a combination bookmark-cum-letter opener, decorated at one end only, usually with a flower (Illus. p. 240).

MONEY HOLDERS

Silver purse frames survive from the 18th century; purses in silver chain mesh from the 19th, when coin holders appeared in America. In novelty forms they held coins of one size, hung from a finger by a chain on a ring attachment.

Baby rattles, Italian mid 17th century.

SMALL COLLECTABLES

MEDALS AND BADGES

A specialist subject, whether the medal given in honor (military etc), badges of identification (badges of office, Admiralty; civic; Livery Companies; domestic servants etc, embossed or engraved with the relevant armorials from very early times), commemorative, either of an event at the time, such as Indian Peace Medals or a battle honor, or honoring a centenary later; sport, (Olympics etc) or any other purpose, in large coin form, suitably embossed.

AMATORY BROOCHES

A form of love token peculiar to Scotland, made in one form or another in all parts, Luckenbooth brooches being peculiar to Edinburgh. Forms include a heart with entwined initials given on betrothal.

COMMEMORATIVE OBJECTS

A silver trowel is often given to commemorate the laying of a corner stone, often engraved, and always inscribed; the spade with which a tree was planted, or the hammer, with which a meeting was called to order are equally usual. Outstanding service, usually recorded on a cup or salver, may take the form of a relevant object, such as a palette for the arts. The scope is unlimited.

Presentation trowel and maul, with ivory handles, Birmingham 1895.

Bookmarkers, *L to R,* American owl, Birmingham 1916; 1946; American 1914, London, 1890; with two sovereign cases, Samson Moroon, 1883, and Birmingham, 1895.

TECHNICAL TERMS

GLOSSARY OF TECHNICAL AND DECORATIVE TERMS

Annealing. The method by which silver under the hammer is kept malleable, by heating on the hearth to about 700°C and then plunging into cold water.

Bright-cut engraving. A form of engraving popular towards the end of the 18th century, which burnishes one side of the cut while picking out the silver with a bevelled edge on the other.

Cast chasing. Used for the improvement of cast ornament, sharpening the design from the front, adding detail and background.

Casting. An ancient method of producing small parts, such as feet, handles or finials. An exact model of the required part is made in a soft material, from which an impression is taken in two halves, forming a mold when clamped together, into which molten silver can be poured.

Chasing. The decoration of silver by the use of punches, removing no silver in the process. This takes several forms.

Chinoiserie. Decoration in the Chinese style, popular throughout Europe, particularly France. (1) copies of Chinese wares such as teapots: (2) Embossing with Chinese figures in the Dutch style: (3) linear decoration in flat chasing, exclusive to England, *c* 1680–90 (referred to as "Chinoiserie" throughout, all else being "in the Chinese style"); (4) repoussé rococo decoration using Chinese motifs, mainly found on objects concerned with tea, *c* 1750 and (5) revivals of any previous Chinese style.

Cut card work. An applied decoration, of French origin popular wherever Huguenots worked, *c* 1660–1730, consisting of flat sections of very thin silver, cut out to a simple pattern such as foliage, and soldered on to the surface of the object to be decorated.

Damascene. An inlay of gold and silver beaten into an undercut groove in another metal, such as copper.

Electro-plating. The application of a pure silver coating to otherwise finished articles, by the process of electrolysis. Perfected by Elkington, *c* 1840.

Electrotyping. A process for making accurate copies of existing work with speed and efficiency.

Embossing. Chasing in relief to any degree, the pattern raised, usually from the back, with rounded punches, capable of producing whole pictures. Indented lines may be embossed from the front.

Cut card work

Chinoiserie

Mouldings:

Ovolu

Egg and dart

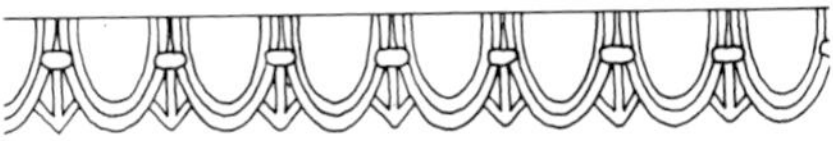

Key pattern

Guilloche

Scrolling foliage

Husk

Diaper pattern

Interlaced strapwork

Laurel festoons

Anathemion

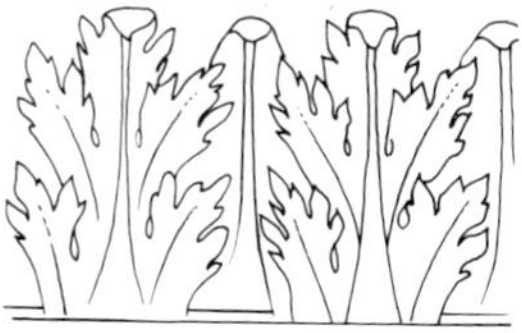

Acanthus

TECHNICAL TERMS

Engraving. Line decoration cut into the surface from the front. Used since primitive times, skill and delicacy of touch are of extreme importance.

Flat chasing. Chasing in very low relief worked from the front, pushing the metal aside in line drawing, giving a less sharply defined, but much more positive, outline than engraving. Always visible from the back.

Gilding. The application of a gold color to silver either (1) by melting gold with mercury and painting it on to the surface with a brush, before removing the mercury by evaporation under heat, causing the two metals to fuse. (2) by soaking a linen rag in a solution of chloride of gold, burning it and rubbing the ashes on to the silver, which adhere, or (3) by modern electrolysis.

Matting. The punching of dots to produce a rough surface; an unburnished surface to provide contrast.

Molding. A border or soldered-on mount, cast or hammered and sometimes pierced.

Niello. A black alloy of silver, copper, lead and sulphur used to fill in engraving, giving an inlaid effect. Used from early times.

Parcel gilt. An object that has been partially gilded.

Planishing. After raising, the object is further hammered with a special tool that smooths out previous hammer marks and corrects any irregularities of thickness or shape.

Raising. The method by which a saucer-shaped circle of silver is hammered up over cast-iron raising stakes, to the desired shape, such as a bowl, keeping the silver evenly distributed, without bubbles, wrinkles or cracks. Frequent annealing is necessary.

Repoussé. The further improvement of embossed decoration, working punches from the front to vary degree, sharpen outline and provide background.

Sheffield plating. A process of fusing silver sheet on to copper before use by the goldsmith. Invented 1743, in full production 1765–1840.

Sinking. The method by which a circle of sheet silver is hammered over a hollow depression in the goldsmith's block (usually an old tree trunk), until it is saucer shaped. A sinking hammer is also used to continue the styling of plates, dishes and other shallow objects.

Soldering. The method by which separately made parts are joined together, using an alloy that will melt at a lower temperature than silver, thereby melting when applied to hot silver during soldering. A hard alloy of

Baluster finial

Pineapple finial

Urn finial

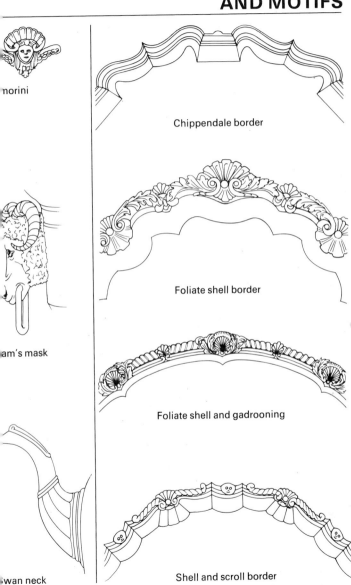

norini

am's mask

wan neck

Chippendale border

Foliate shell border

Foliate shell and gadrooning

Shell and scroll border

TECHNICAL TERMS

silver and zinc is now generally used. A flux of borax dissolves oxides over the area, so improving the effective hold of the solder.

Spinning. The production of hollow wares on a spinning lathe by means of forcing a disc of rotating silver up around a previously hand turned hard wood head, with a long-handled steel headed tool, until it has taken its likeness. Known since ancient times, but popular since the early 19th century.

Stamping. The mechanical production of "ready-made" parts in quantity, complete with their decoration, by the use of hard steel dies, cut in reverse to the required pattern, from *c* 1820. Stamped borders, strapwork etc used from the 16th century, were hand hammered from the back, also using hand-cut dies.

Swaging. Decorative wires and hand-forged spoons were produced by hammering hot or cold metal over a groove called a swage.

Wire drawing. A method by which silver rod is drawn through ever diminishing holes to the required thickness (with constant annealing), down to a hair's breadth for filigree. Machines, introduced *c* 1770 perform the same process mechanically and are also able to produce beaded and other ornamental wires. These had previously been made by either hammering over a grooved block or shaped die, or by casting.

Ball and claw foot
with foliate supports

Pedestal base

Scroll foot

Dolphin foot

Shell foot with shell knuckle

Sphinx

on mask and ring

Figural handle

Loop handle

atyr

Flying scroll handle

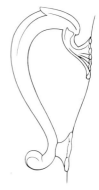

Double scroll handle

Winged griffon

Harp handle

Pierced lug handle

SILVER MARKS

SILVER MARKS

Silver marks are a valuable means of identifying the date and origin of antique silver but marks of very similar appearance may have very different significance in different places and care must be taken in reading them to ensure accuracy. A number of reference books cataloguing marks are available and should be consulted when identification is required: some are listed in the bibliography. In Britain a pamphlet giving assay marks and date letters in England and Scotland up to the present day is issued by the assay offices and available on request to anyone sending a stamped, self-addressed envelope, size 4in × 9in, to their local assay office. Silver dealers may also have copies available.

Special marks have been authorized since 1976 to be used as approved hallmarks under an international convention at assay offices in the United Kingdom, Austria, Finland, Sweden and Switzerland. They consist of a sponsor's mark, a common control mark, a fineness mark (arabic numerals showing the standard in parts per thousand) and an assay office mark. They do not include a date letter.

In many other countries marks used on precious metals are struck by the manufacturer and do not indicate an independent certification, they do however, greatly aid in identification of the piece, if not guaranteeing the quality of the metal.

Britain is the only country with a clearly worked out and consistent system of marks on antique silver. Dutch silver, especially that of Amsterdam, has a similar marking system, but its full use was not enforced. For

Top row:
Marks from a piece by Paul Lamerie, London 1716. First comes the Britannia silver mark, followed by the year mark of the London assay office, then the lion's head erased and finally the maker's mark which, at this period, had to include the first two letters of the maker's surname.

Center row:
Marks from a piece by Matthew Boulton, 1798, consist of the lion passant; the Birmingham assay office mark of an anchor, the date letter, the sovereign's head duty mark for George III (duty marks were used 1784–1890 in Britain) and the maker's mark.

Bottom row:
Marks from a piece made by Hendrik Swiering, Amsterdam, 1755, consist of maker's mark, town mark, mark of the province and year letter.

SILVER MARKS

other countries various marks, indicating fineness and payment of excise duty appear, but their use is not consistent enough to be a reliable aid to identification. Town marks were used in almost every European silver center, indicating place of origin and, where changes occurred in the symbol used, giving a rough indication of date: the Irish harp crowned and Hibernia marks, for example, changed in detail yearly.

In Britain, where marks have been used since 1300, a leopard's head (a lion's face) is the London sterling mark, also used as proof of assay in most English provincial offices. A lion passant (sideways walking) is the London standard mark, also used in most English provincial centers; this is replaced by a thistle in

American goldsmiths' marks frequently consist simply of the maker's name. They also sometimes took the form of initials in shields or other symbols more like European marks, as in some of these examples.

 John Coney (Boston) 1655–1722

 Timothy Dwight (Boston) 1654–91

 Samuel Edwards (Boston) 1705–62

 Henry Evans (New York) c 1820

 Richard Humphreys (Philadelphia) advertised 1771–96

 Elias Pelletreau (Southampton, NY) 1726–1810

 Paul Revere (Boston) 1735–1818

 Joseph Richardson (Philadelphia) 1711–84

SILVER MARKS

Edinburgh, a lion rampant in Glasgow or a harp in Dublin. A lion's head erased when in conjunction with a figure of Britannia indicates that the silver is of the higher standard (95.8 per cent, compulsory 1697–1720 and optional thereafter), stamped in London only 1697–1701, and York, Chester and Exeter from 1701, and Newcastle from 1702.

The word "Sterling" would indicate American silver after 1860, or Cork or Limerick in Ireland c 1710–84, although the stamping of this word did have many other connotations, mostly rare. In all cases it indicates the sterling standard of 92.5 per cent silver.

Ornate capital letters with a crown or fleur-de-lis often indicate that a piece is French, and a spread eagle

Various European fineness and other marks.

 Standard mark 925 (sterling) quality London c 1600

 Standard mark 925 quality Ireland

 Standard mark 925 quality Edinburgh

 Standard mark 800 quality Belgium 18th century

 Standard mark 833 quality Netherlands since 1852

 Standard mark 950 quality Austria 1866–72

 Standard mark 950 quality Italy 1873–1935

 Sovereign's head duty mark for Queen Victoria, Britain 1836–90

 Guarantee mark for medium-sized items, Paris 1798–1809

 Review mark, France 1809 medium-sized item

 French import mark 1893

 Austrian exemption mark 1809–10 (exempt from consignment to state treasury)

TOWN MARKS

 Amsterdam (Netherlands) *c* 1566 18th century

Antwerp (Belgium) 16th and 17th century

 Augsburg (Germany) 17th and two 18th century

  Basle (Switzerland) 17th–18th and 18th century

Bergen (Norway) 18th–19th centuries

 Berlin (Germany) Early and late 18th century

  Berne (Switzerland) 16th and 18th century

Birmingham (England)

 Bruges (Belgium) 17th century

Brussels (Belgium) all 18th century

 Budapest (Hungary) pre 1800 and 1810–65

Chester (England) 18th century and from 1780

 Cologne (German) End 17th and end 18th centuries

Copenhagen (Denmark) from 1608

 Cork (Ireland) both 17th–q8th centuries

Cordova (Spain) 15th–16th centuries

 Dordrecht (Netherlands) 18th century

 Dresden (Germany) 19th century

 Edinburgh (Scotland) 16th–17th centuries and from 1760

 Exeter (England) 1575–1698 and 1701–19th century

 Ferrara (Italy) 17th century

 Florence (Italy) 17th–18th and 18th centuries

 Gdansk (Danzig, Poland) 17th–18th centuries

 Geneva (Switzerland) 18th century

 Genoa (Italy) 17th–18th centuries

 Ghent (Belgium) Both 18th century

 Haarlem (Netherlands) 18th century

 Hamburg (Germany) 17th–18th centuries

 Irkutsk (USSR) 1777–89 and 1815–25

 Kiev (USSR) 1735–74 and 1848–65

TOWN MARKS

 Leyden (Netherlands)
18th century

 Liege (Belgium)
18th century

 Lisbon (Portugal)
17th–18th and
18th–19th centuries

 Luneburg (Germany)
16th–17th centuries
and since 1800

 Madrid (Spain)
18th century

 Moscow (Russia)
1740 and 1780

 Munich (Germany)
c 1700 and
1762–1860

 Naples (Italy)
17th–18th and 18th
centuries

 Neuchatel (Switzerland)
1820–66

 Newcastle (England)
from 1672

 Nuremberg (Germany)
1700–50 and 19th
century

 Oslo (Norway)
1642–c 1820

 Paris (France)
Both 1684–7

 Prague (Czechoslovakia)
1666–76 and
1793–1806

 Rome (Italy)
17th–18th and late
17th centuries

 Rotterdam (Nether
lands) 18th cen

 St Petersburg
(Leningrad, US
end 19th centu

 Salzburg (Aust
18th century

 Sheffield (Engl
from 1773

 Stockholm (Sw
16th–17th and
centuries

 Stuttgart (Germ
18th–19th and
centuries

 Toulouse (Fran
16th–17th and
centuries

 Turin (Italy)
from 1678 and
century

 Utrecht (Nether
18th century

 Venice (Italy)
17th–18th cent

Viborg (Denma
17th–18th cent

 Vienna (Austria)
1691–1737 and
1784–1806

Ypres (Belgium)
End 17th centur
1701–13

Zurich (Switzerl
17th and 17th–1
centuries

Zwolle (Netherla
18th century

252

is often a sign of German origin, although there are other sources which also used these symbols—the eagle for instance was a symbol used by Russia and throughout the Hapsburg empire.

The variety of silver marks is so wide that it requires considerable knowledge and exhaustive reference sources to be sure of an identification of many marks. The examples given may help the reader appreciate the problems and lead him in the right direction, but if a positive identification is required more detailed sources should be consulted or expert advice sought. Silver dealers and auction houses will usually be happy to give advice whether or not an object is being offered for sale.

BIBLIOGRAPHY

Judith Banister, *An Introduction to Old English Silver,* Evans, 1965

Douglas Bennet, *Irish Georgian Silver,* Cassell, 1972

F. Bradbury, *Book of Hallmarks,* Northend, 1975

Richard Came, *Silver,* Weidenfeld and Nicholson, 1961

Michael Clayton, *The Collector's Dictionary of the Silver and Gold of Great Britain and North America,* Country Life/World Publishing Co., 1971

Frank Davis, *French Silver,* Arthur Barker, 1970

Eric Delieb, *Investing in Silver,* Cassell, 1972

Jan Divis, *Silver Marks of the World,* Hamlyn, 1976

Ian Harris, *Price Guide to Antique Silver,* Antique Collectors Club, 1969

John Hayward, *Huguenot Silver in England,* Faber, 1959

Graham Hood, *American Silver,* Praeger, 1971

Michael Snodin, *English Silver Spoons,* Letts, 1974

Gerald Taylor, *Silver,* Penguin, 1956; *Continental Gold and Silver,* Michael Joseph, 1967

Seymour B. Wyler, *The Book of Old Silver* (contains many silver marks), Crown, 1937

INDEX

INDEX